Freshly Squeezed

Freshly Squeezed

A
"Write Here, Write Now"
Anthology

Edited by
Christine Stewart

Apprentice House
Baltimore, Maryland

Library of Congress Cataloging-in-Publication Data

Freshly squeezed : a Write Here, Write Now anthology /
edited by Christine Stewart.
p. cm.
ISBN 978-1-934074-32-9
1. American literature--Maryland--Baltimore. 2. American
literature--21st century. I. Stewart, Christine, 1966-

PS559.B3F73 2008
810.8'097526--dc22
2007051087

Printed in the United States of America

Cover photograph features comfort food at
Broadway Diner, 6501 Eastern Avenue
Baltimore, MD 21224

Published by Apprentice House
The Future of Publishing…Today!

Apprentice House
Communication Department
Loyola College in Maryland
4501 N. Charles Street
Baltimore, MD 21210
410.617.5265 • 410.617.5040 (fax)
www.ApprenticeHouse.com

"Every man, when he gets quiet, when he becomes desperately honest with himself, is capable of uttering profound truths. We all derive from the same source. There is no mystery about the origin of things. We are all part of creation, all kings, all poets, all musicians; we have only to open up, only to discover what is already there."

—Henry Miller

Write Here, Write Now

The pieces in this anthology came out of the "Write Here, Write Now" workshops held throughout the year at the Creative Alliance in Baltimore, Maryland. The workshops formed from the partnership between Christine Stewart, Creator of the WHWN series; Jed Dodds, Artistic Director for Creative Alliance; and Gregg Wilhelm, Executive Director of CityLit Project.

For more information about the workshops, go to www.whwnwriters.com. For information on the partners/sponsors:

Christine Stewart — www.therealwriter.com

Creative Alliance — www.creativealliance.org

CityLit Project — www.citylitproject.org

If you are a local writer, you'll find even more information about Baltimore's writing community at the website of the Maryland Writers' Association's Baltimore Chapter (www.mwabaltimore.org).

Table of Contents

10 MINUTE PLAYS

POETRY

FICTION

Introduction

It is hard to believe the "Write Here, Write Now" program is only three years old. We have come such a long way in such a short time, due in no small part to our sponsors (Creative Alliance and CityLit Project), our venue (at Creative Alliance), and the dozens of enthusiastic, committed, and talented writers who keep coming back to share their vision with us, and spread the word about our classes. What started as a community has become more like a writing family, and it's growing every day.

Our goal was to create a safe, supportive, yet challenging environment for writers to develop their voice and skills in a non-academic setting. To provide everything one would learn in a college classroom, without the grades, the credits, and the costs, but with extra attention and care, and to address not just writing, but the *writing life*. We had big dreams: a wide range of classes, readings, festivals, theatrical events, gallery shows, interaction with the media, salons, and they all came true. What a terrific task to now be faced with —dreaming even bigger!

In this, the first anthology from participants of WHWN, you'll find a solid, surprising, and varied body of work—poems, 10-minute plays, essays, memoir and novel excerpts, and short stories. You'll read pieces crafted with patience and love by writers dedicated to exploring the depth and breadth of their skills and their subjects. You'll be moved, as we were, by their honesty and their passion.

We didn't know what would happen when we started this program. Now we know that if we had any expectations, the writers of WHWN far exceeded them. We want to say thank you for allowing us to be part of your evolution. We're looking forward to another amazing year of discovery.

We'd like to heartily thank each other for a job well done and a wonderful partnership. Thanks to Creative Alliance and CityLit Project for their enthusiastic and unwavering support. Thanks also to Apprentice House for its thoughtful stewardship of this book from beginning to end. You've made a lot of writers very happy!

We'd also like to thank you for supporting local writers by purchasing this anthology. If you're not already a member of our community, consider joining us. As the neon-sign logo suggests, WHWN is a welcoming community. Come on in!

Chris, Jed, and Gregg

Nonfiction

Kick Ass Mujeres

Manisha Gadia

Whenever I need some kick ass women to remind me that I kick ass, I listen to my "kick ass mujeres" playlist. *Mujeres* means "women" in Spanish. The raw, brazen, guttural *j* sound in *mujeres* seems to capture the aspects of femininity elucidated by this playlist better than the word woman. I created this playlist about a year ago, and while its contents have changed, I'm still satisfied with the title. I've used lowercase letters because the title comes on strong enough without capitalizing it. 'Kick Ass Mujeres,' capitalized, is too formal and not playful enough, whereas "kick ass mujeres" seems more appropriate to its producer: young, vibrant, bold, but not rah-rah like a cheerleader. Originally, the playlist included over twenty songs, and ultimately I've selected the following seven songs by seven women because they represent varying aspects of femininity, and together embody what being a woman means to me.

"Express Yourself"
by Madonna
Don't go for second best baby
Put your love to the test
You know, you know, you've got to
Make him express how he feels
And maybe then you'll know your love is real

This is a fantastic anthem about not settling. I feel

increasingly squeezed inside a vise that creates pressure for me to hurry up and find the guy I am going to marry, because it is the right thing to do, because I am at that age, because getting settled will supposedly secure my happiness, and because people in my life want to throw a fabulous party. While in this vise, I debate whether to accept my two-dimensional fate or whether to push back and try not to get flattened. The incessant cranking makes it difficult to know how I really feel. Do I even want to get married? Asking questions might make me implode before the vise closes in completely.

What you need is a big strong hand
To lift you to your higher ground

Madonna's voice lifts me to my higher ground, out of the vise just before it squishes me completely. On this higher ground, I can be okay with who I am, and I have enough air to breathe so I can ask questions and find my own answers.

You deserve the best in life
So if the time isn't right then move on
Second best is never enough
You'll do much better baby on your own

Listening to Madonna won't doom me to permanent singledom, but it might help prevent permanent 'two-dementia' brought on by fear of the alternative.

"Resham Ka Roomal"
by Ila Arun

Resham ka ha! Resham ka roomal gale pe daal ke, tum aaja na...

Essentially, the meaning of this Hindi song can be boiled down to: *Come to me, I'm waiting, and I'm hot for you.* A more literal translation: *Come to me wearing a silk handkerchief around your neck, lover of mine. I've made myself up with Delhi kohl and I've been waiting at the door. I've fallen for you, the looks you give me make me crazy. I'm all decked out wearing my nose ring, my toe rings, my red stole, clinking anklets, and a ring of jasmine flowers in my hair. Put a linen shirt on your body and come to me; you'll be chewing Banaras tobacco when you come. I've been waiting, waiting for so long at the door*

Although Ila Arun's fantasy is fully-clothed, the tone of her husky voice, the horn instruments used to charm snakes, and the bells and drums used to charm men leave little doubt as to the singer's lustful desire.

When does sexuality become okay for an Indian woman? The obvious answer would be after marriage, and directed only at one's husband, but even then it's covert. We must rely on suggestive lyrics and physical adornments: jewelry, makeup, colorful clothing. Our innuendos must be those of a tamed tigress: a midriff-baring sari blouse translucently covered by a sheer chiffon sari is perfectly okay, but a sleeveless sari blouse could be overly suggestive.

Resham ka Roomal is a song loved by every Indian woman I know. Although I can comfortably discuss the implicit meaning of the song with my peers, the fact that this song is also a favorite among my mother and her peers makes me wonder what they love about it. I know that part of its appeal is its folksy sensibility and unique sound that contrasts with the usual ultra soprano female falsetto usually heard in popular Hindi music. Yet I also suspect that every woman I know likes it because it is sexy and makes her feel sexy when she dances along to it.

As an adolescent, I danced to this song on stage with a group of my female peers. Most of the choreography was acting out the literal meaning of the lyrics. I remember our moms helping us choose and vetoing dance songs for performances at Indian cultural functions. (Once a song that my friends and I chose was vetoed because it was too racy—it included heavy breathing if I remember correctly). Yet somehow I think *Resham ka Roomal* would never have been vetoed; in fact it was probably chosen by one of our mothers. Although I didn't consider the full depth of its sexiness until recently, I knew this song was sexy the first time I heard it and have loved it ever since.

"Take Me or Leave Me"
As sung by characters Maureen and Joanne in *Rent*
Take me for what I am
Who I was meant to be
And if you give a damn
Take me baby or leave me

In the musical *Rent*, Maureen is Mark's ex-girlfriend and now she's dating a woman named Joanne. This song is a fight between Maureen and Joanne, each asking the other to accept her as she is. Although the song is mainly about a relationship struggle, it also explores sexual identity and our need for acceptance and love.

...everybody stares at me,
Boys, girls, I can't help it baby...
A tiger in a cage can never see the sun
This diva needs her stage,
Baby - let's have fun!

I seem to attract attention from across the gender and sexual identity spectrum: gay men, lesbians, bisexual men and women, and straight men and women. My sense is that this a little unusual, although I don't know if it's that I'm more aware of this attention than other people are or if it's something about me. I suppose that it is a little of both.

Since a young age, I have seen gay rights as a civil and human rights issue, and I have strived to educate myself on gender and sexual identity. There was no one incident or person that compelled me to feel strongly about this, but a number of things I've learned along the way have strengthened my resolve. Becoming more aware of cultural biases towards heterosexuality and clear-cut gender identity, along with improving my "gaydar," has allowed me to see the world and its complexities more fully. I believe that my openness to myself and others, and my willingness to learn makes a variety of people comfortable around me. Thankfully, my openness has allowed me to have diversity in my life, including a number of friends with sexual orientations different from my own.

So, again, the attention I get is a mix of my awareness of the attention, and something about my personality and the exuberant vibe I radiate. Oh dear, I think I'm sounding a little conceited. It's fitting though, "this diva needs her stage"! I am beginning to realize what an attention-fiend I am. Recently when at a gay bar, a hottie hetero girl complained to me that she doesn't mind gay people but that no guys were, like, checking her out. I nodded blankly; trying not to roll my eyes rudely at her, and thought to myself *gay men LOVE me!* I walked away from her and immediately approached a guy on the dance floor and danced with him. Carpe diem!

"If He Tries Anything"
by Ani DiFranco

It was difficult to choose only one Ani DiFranco song, there are many that fit the mood and theme of this playlist. Her lyrics seem to express my feminine angst with astonishing precision. I chose *If He Tries Anything* because it captures female camaraderie, and challenges the "rules" women feel we should follow.

I'm invincible
So are you
We do all the things
They say we can't do
We walk around
In the middle of the night
And if it's too far to walk
We just hitch a ride

I know I am not invincible. In mid-September of

2005, less than a month after moving to Baltimore, I was maced for no apparent reason. A young man to whom I posed no threat pepper-sprayed me in the face just after I crossed the street by my apartment at 9 p.m. on a Friday night. I started screaming because there were people close by dining outside a restaurant down the block who would hear me, and because there was little else my shaking, burning body would allow me to do. Thankfully, he disappeared once I started screaming and never touched me; but it would have been easy for him to mug me or rape me. The police report I filed a couple weeks later classified the incident as an "aggravated assault," giving credence to the seriousness of it.

Perhaps this incident should have made me move to somewhere "safer," fear walking anywhere alone, and never leave the house after dark. But it didn't. Why not? Part of it is stupid stubbornness. Part of it is a sense that what happened to me could have happened to anyone, any time, anywhere. I know I am not invincible, but not making my decisions based on fear, and not following rules just because I'm supposed to makes me feel invincible.

It's a long long road
It's a big big world
We are wise wise women
We are giggling girls
We both carry a smile
To show when we're pleased
We both carry a switchblade
In our sleeves

In the past few years, women close to me have dealt with divorce, cheating husbands, job discrimination, sexual harassment, abortion, infertility, breast cancer, and heartbreak. These events have demonstrated female vulnerability, resilience, and strength. To be sure, there were often men in our lives that helped us through these things. Yet I believe that these women, including myself, leaned on the understanding and compassion of other women to move forward in our lives.

I say I think he likes you
You say I think he do too
I say go and get him girl
Before he gets you
I'll be watching you
From the window
I will come to your rescue
If he tries anything

We are there for each other, cheering each other on and cushioning each other's fall as we break rules and live life.

"Sunshowers"
by M.I.A.
I salt and pepper my mango

M.I.A. is a skinnier, taller, sexier, more badass version of me. She's like my hot older sister. My brother introduced me to her music by sending me a link to one of her music videos. Shortly thereafter I bought her CD *Arular.* The song "Sunshowers" initially caught my attention because I liked the line "I salt and pepper my mango," a tribute to her ethnicity and a statement I could relate to. In the dining hall at college, I would often salt and pepper my orange juice to get a rise out of my dinnermates, but also because it tastes good.

Semi-9 and snipered him
On that wall they posted him
They cornered him
and then just murdered him ....
He had Colgate on his teeth
And Reebok classics on his feet
At a factory he does Nike
And then helps the family

As I learned more about M.I.A., I became even more fascinated with her. M.I.A. was part of the Tamil ethnic minority in Sri Lanka. She was born in London but her family moved to Sri Lanka when she was an infant, and her father became a revolutionary fighting for the Tamil separatist movement. Civil War broke out in Sri Lanka and she and her mother and her siblings escaped Sri Lanka, to India, and then on to London where they lived as refugees. In addition to her music, M.I.A. is a talented graffiti-inspired artist and overall extremely creative person. I don't know enough about her politics to know whether I agree with her views, but it stirs something within me when people stand up and fight for their beliefs in the face of adversity. According to Wikipedia, the video for "Sunshowers" is censored by MTV because it makes a reference to the P.L.O.

and M.I.A. has been denied visas to visit to the U.S. and Canada.

I bongo with my lingo
Beat it like a wing yo
From Congo to Columbo
Can't stereotype my thing yo

My admiration of M.I.A. prompts me to embrace my own strengths. She's South Asian, beautiful, creative, and outspoken. She's famous and I like what she has contributed to the world. All these qualities make her a sort of peer role model.

"When You're Good To Mama"
As sung by Queen Latifah in *Chicago*

They say that life is tit for tat
And that's the way I live
So, I deserve a lot of tat
For what I've got to give
Don't you know that this hand
Washes that one too
When you're good to Mama
Mama's good to you!

Queen Latifah is 100% bootylicious and she isn't afraid to flaunt it. I guess part of what makes someone "bootylicious" is part voluptuousness part flaunt factor. What human wouldn't be turned on by that coquettish smile and confrontational cleavage?

Unwavering confidence and a positive body image are tenuous possessions for many women, particularly when we believe we should swallow sentences like: "You're pretty but you would be a bombshell if you went to the gym and ran three miles everyday." Yes, a guy I dated actually said that to me, and yes, I failed to break up him with immediately. I waited until he destroyed my confidence a little bit more, and eventually it dawned on me that his constructive criticisms were not all that constructive.

If you want my gravy
Pepper my ragout
Spice it up for Mama
She'll get hot for you

I saw the Hollywood movie version of *Chicago* first and later saw it on Broadway. Although I enjoyed both, I thought the movie more powerfully captured the highly feminine, libidinous undertones of the musical. In particular I was struck by Queen Latifah, who is clearly beautiful but does not fit the conventional standard for beauty. Beauty is not about body type!

"Bewitched, Bothered, and Bewildered" by Ella Fitzgerald
Men are not a new sensation
I've done pretty well I think
But this half-pint imitation
Put me on the blink
I'm wild again, beguiled again
A simpering, whimpering child again
Bewitched, bothered and bewildered—am I

Although I didn't really start listening to Ella Fitzgerald's music until high school or college, I've felt a loyalty to her since seventh grade when I was assigned to do a report on her for music class. The piano, gentle percussion, bass, and the richness of Ella Fitzgerald's voice make this song elegant and languid.

"Bewitched, Bothered, and Bewildered" is about the lifecycle of relationships, the hope and renewed confidence that arise from a new infatuation, and the discovery of fluttery feelings when you are not expecting them.

Lost my heart, but what of it

I am the girl of intense crushes. I let myself fall rather than protect my heart too carefully. My heart does break, but it also heals, and my faith that I will be bewitched, bothered, and bewildered again is never shattered permanently.

Madonna, Ila Arun, "Maureen," Ani DiFranco, M.I.A., Queen Latifah, and Ella Fitzgerald represent a wide range of musical styles: pop, Indian, Broadway, alternative rock, eclectic hip hop, jazz. They are strong, they are feminine, and they are candid. Listening to this playlist reminds me that it's okay for me to have these qualities as well. While the list is composed of my personal choices, I think these songs would have a similar empowering effect on other women who need to be reminded that they kick ass!

Manisha Gadia kicks ass.

Judith Regan, Age, Dario

Barbara Friedland

Judith Regan. Where to begin? Let's start at the end. The fact that she was unceremoniously fired, and escorted out of the building, is interesting. The reason? Get this: she made anti-Semitic statements. Really? In the business world? Hard to believe. I will be willing to wager that this is not the first time that this famous editor uttered such sentiments.

Frankly, if everyone was fired for bias or prejudice, the workplaces and executive offices would look like the desert. Dry and abandoned with sagebrush being tossed by the wind. Some of the statements that Regan said were printed in the newspapers and they are mild. References to a Jewish cabal and such. Frankly, after the Mel Gibson tirade and the recent Holocaust denier conference in Iraq, it seemed almost inconsequential.

Let's face it, Regan was fired for the O.J. Simpson debacle. Which is like shooting the messenger. I am pretty certain that she did not murder Nicole Brown Simpson and Ronald Goldman. It is documented that she wasn't on the jury for the criminal trial that acquitted him. Nor was she a member of the prosecution team that lost. What she did was ideate the convoluted project of how to generate money for O.J., and get him back in front of television cameras. The public, whoever they may be, spoke loudly and convincingly. They did not want to hear how this man may have allegedly killed those two innocent people. Many believe that they already know.

The problem with business today is that, besides being corrupt, it has ossified into fearful arenas where employees are not encouraged to come up with new and different concepts. I worked for a marketing firm for two months. (It seemed much longer.) Every innovative idea I had was ridiculed or ignored. Even relatively benign concepts were eschewed—fearfully I might add. Through the power of the Internet, I was able to discern the newly appointed VP of Marketing for a local sports equipment company, specializing in shoes and other athletic gear. I suggested writing him, sending some collateral and enclosing a chocolate foot. Nicely packaged and hygienic, the candy would be an usual and different missive from the many he must receive on a daily basis. Worst case scenario, he eats the chocolate and doesn't do business with us—no different than the present situation. Or his interest is piqued and he begins to interact with the company.

Frankly reaction by the owners of my company was steadfastly opposed. The level of their response was like I'd suggested sending anthrax.

The largest advertising agency in Baltimore recently went out of business, leaving several major clients needing services. There was clearly an heir apparent, poised to take over all or most of the orphaned accounts. I merely suggested talking with that company, offering complementary services and working together. Again, the response was immediate and harsh.

Even ideas that in retrospect are stupid should be given credit for launch and execution. Okay, Sony tried to pass a flog (fake blog) as authentic gamers actually writing. Dumb? Maybe. If it had worked, it would have been brilliant. Did anyone die? Was a new war started? No. Sony simply has to find a more effective way to communicate to consumers.

Innovation is being strangled by corporate cowardice. There is no room for error any more. People are being more cautious and the result is business as usual.

I will give some advice to Judith Regan: you are clearly an innovator and strong personality. Not all of your ideas will be successful, especially since they are sometimes radically different than the status quo. So in the wake of a temporary set back, lay low and speak nice. Act contrite and cooperative for awhile, until the incident has blown over or you have just engineered an undeniable homerun. Then plan your next victory.

Age

Age, specifically the passing of years, snuck up on me not once, but twice. The first time was when I realized that my mother was old. (The other circumstance is a story for another day.) I knew for quite awhile but would not admit it to myself. Just like the time I wanted to skip the memorial for my college friend, felled by breast cancer. To stay home meant that she wasn't gone. In my version, we could co-exist and simply not see each other.

My mother showed signs of age and deterioration long before I moved her to Baltimore. My father died very young, at 62. He was vibrant and alive until struck by a rare disease diagnosed far too late. He slipped into illness and then death. Dad was never old. After he died, my mother soldiered on. She stayed active and involved. At the expense of her own health, she nursed her sister until she passed on, just as she'd done for Dad and my grandmother before that. The birth of my son, Jonathan (The Second Coming as it's known in my family), renewed my mother's spirit. She stayed in touch from New Jersey, taping television shows that she thought he would enjoy. Each visit cemented their relationship.

Finally, my brothers and I convinced her to sell the house, the only home she had since her marriage. She raised three children and loved her husband there. Her achievements—getting a master's degree and starting a teaching career—echoed throughout the universe, both there and finally in Maryland. Reluctantly she put the house on the market and probably sold it for far too little money. At this point her mind was slipping. Just a little.

By the time she came to visit and house hunt here, she was in health distress. My friend, a doctor, saw her several times in a fortnight period. She finally put my mother on a waiting list for a hospital bed. We, my mother and I, went out to eat and enjoyed the time. The call letting us know that there was space for her came later that evening. As I drove to the hospital, she had a heart attack.

She remained hospitalized for more than ten days, during a time when insurance companies were very stringent about costs. She was not herself; she was very nasty to me and Jonathan—an aberration that has never occurred before or since. My friend, her doctor, and my brother, who lived here in Maryland, wanted to put her into assisted living. She told me that she would stop eating if forced to live in such a place. I thought that argument trumped everything else. I found a wonderful apartment surrounded by lush lawns and foliage. Her unit looked like a little house, and sat at the very tip of the huge complex, making finding it very easy. It was a duplex, but my mother's hearing, the diminishing aural acuity, prevented her from being disturbed, or even aware of the upstairs neighbor. Sitting at the dining room table, a shopping complex loomed into view a very few, short blocks away.

My brother went and packed up the house in New Jersey. I took my mother to see the apartment. She loved it and we planned to return the following day to sign a lease. That day she almost had a stroke. Not quite that, but one or two small events that disturbed brain and motor function. I called my friend, her doctor, frantically. By the time the ambulance arrived, my mother was fine. She was insulted when the driver asked her to identify the current president. This time she answered correctly. Usually she just quoted my son, saying it was Monica Lewinsky's friend.

So again my mother was hospitalized and then convalesced at my house. She hated losing her independence and despised the city. She longed for trees and grass, spaces between house and a slower, quieter atmosphere. Finally after a month, I called the apartment complex. The very apartment that we both loved was still vacant. She moved in later that week.

I prayed daily that she be safe and happy. No home invasions or horrific accidents. I was forced to hire a woman to supervise her medication regime. And a cleaning lady. And a masseuse. The latter two were my pleasure and my mother's. She would walk to the nearby supermarket several times a day. My son and I would visit frequently. Because of our renovation, he would often have sleepover parties at her apartment. Sometimes, it would be just him spending the night.

One day I went and there was no food in the refrigerator. I'd been used to her kitchen overflowing with things to eat. The cleaning lady would have to throw away bags and bags of spoiled victuals. The present situation only meant one thing. My mother was not walking the short distance to the shopping center. I started coming weekly and shopping for her, stocking up on nutritious things as well as treats that she loved. Sadly, she was hospitalized once, then again. Her mind continued to deteriorate. It was clear that she could not live alone. She moved in with my brother in Rockville.

For a year, she begged me to take her home. This time it meant her apartment in Maryland, not her house in New Jersey. Every time I visited, she started packing, hoping to leave.

She is still with my brother and his family. She loves it when my son visits, but cannot remember his name. She barely notices her other three grandchildren, who are her daily companions. For years, she has only eaten ice cream, cookies and eggs. At first, I was highly critical of the situation. I went to visit and took her out to dinner. Ordering all her favorites, salmon, broccoli and soup, my mother just looked at the plate. Finally we ordered a milkshake so she could ingest something. I packed up the meal, took it back and left it for my brother.

I could never repay her for all that she has done for me. I believe that one small gift was my insistence that she have her own place. Those five precious years in the apartment.

Dario

Dario has been very helpful recently. And funny. Dario Gino is the father of my son. And he does not have one ounce of Italian blood in him. His parents' names are Dorothy and Roy. He actually looks like his heritage, which is an amalgam of Western Europe, a little American Indian, and one Jewish grandparent. The term often used for someone with his visage is Black Irish. Pale skin, blue eyes, and dark hair.

Our son looks a lot like him and resembles me somewhat, but we, his parents, do not favor each other. We look like a couple, that's all.

Back to the name. Dario's mother flirts with the exotic and high drama. I believe she was watching the Academy Awards when she went into labor. (There is a famous Italian producer, Dario Fo.) It's unclear where she actually found this name and she continues to this day, to be intentionally vague on the subject. And then, in an attempt at ethnic symmetry, she used a middle name that she felt "fit." Dario is relatively uncommon in Italy. I visited friends in Milan just as we started dating. I thought I would bring him some personalized items, a feat impossible to achieve here in the United States. Just as difficult there. Looking at toothbrushes, wallets, and other things, I saw "Mario" embroidered or printed on merchandise in each store, but never the name I wanted.

Dario actually loves his name. Although it belies his heritage, it is unique and interesting. People remember it and he is always the only one. There was never a question that we would use it for his son. I am Jewish and we honor the deceased by naming the baby after a relative who is gone. Although I was close to killing Dario at the time, he was very much alive and well. Also, combined, Dario and I have zero percent Italian heritage. It was silly to use an appellation so ethnic.

I wanted to name my son Kermit after my father. Unfortunately, the Muppets happened. The frog. Kermit. Prior to that, and even after the popularity of Sesame Street, my father loved his name. Kermit Roosevelt was President Roosevelt's eldest soon—Teddy not Franklin. For some reason, the name spread like wildfire in my family. My dad had two cousins sharing it. Still, friends took my grandmother to task. She was an immigrant living in the United States. What kind of name was that to give to her son, her child that would assimilate here? She had one more offspring, another boy, and she named him Joe. As in *GI* and *I will have a cuppa*. What could be more red, white, and blue? Of course, he was the one who was teased throughout school—called Josephine and such—while my father, Kermit, skated along.

So my son's name is Jonathan Kermit. I couldn't have called him my father's name. I don't know how Gentiles do it. Some families have a whole set of people with the same name and then some type of identification. As in Jr., or Little or numbers following it.

Back to Dario. He and I have gotten closer as our

son has grown. Of course Jonathan is exactly the child that his father envisioned. I don't have to explain poetry camp or a passion for Broadway musicals. Our kid, who is athletic, handsome, and popular, is interested in all types of sports and has a trail of girls after him. As I stated, just what his father wanted and can relate to.

Since money has been very tight for the last couple years, Dario has stepped up and paid for all the important high school expenses that I could not afford. Prom, wrestling camp, letterman jacket, school ring. He provides health insurance. The two participate in fantasy football together, with dad paying for his son's league fees. He buys groceries and goes to wrestling matches and baseball games.

Without a soap rendition of the early years, this is a major transformation. Believe me. Dario does not make much money and has contributed far more than I would have expected. He also can be wise and funny.

Recently, both of us went to a match. Jonathan is now captain of the wrestling team. For the previous two years, he was in the heavyweight division. Now his weight class is 215. These are generally much better athletes, more fit and faster. Sometimes, heavyweight wrestlers are very fat kids put on the team so the coach would not have to forfeit that category. Jonathan dispensed them with ease. Two-fifteen is another story. These guys are football players who have just left the gym after lifting weights for their entire lives.

At the match last week, we watched as the opposing wrestler walked into the circle to face our child. He was huge. His legs looked like tree stumps. I was silently praying that Jonathan not be hurt. Dario turned to me and said, "See how this kid is cut. It looks like he just got out of prison." (For my writing group, cut in this context means that his muscles were well defined through extensive weight training. And in my opinion, enough steroids to make Barry Bonds ill.)

And so it goes. Jonathan is acting up a little and I get discouraged. Dario brings reassurance and a broader view. Seventeen years ago, my family wanted him out of my life. I am so glad he is still here.

See Barbara's other piece, an excerpt from her novel, A Member of the Force, *in the fiction section of this anthology.*

I'm Doing Well, Considering

Charles Myers

Recently, I told Dave, my stepfather, that I am doing pretty well, considering. He responded, "Yes… considering." He'd gotten out of prison four months earlier, for breaking parole in 2002. During his three-and-a-half-year sentence, I kept his dog, paid his bills with his retirement income, and sent him money orders for the commissary account. His original parole deal was one year for fondling a twelve-year-old boy, which he said he never did.

Although it's been a long, continuous effort I'm doing pretty well and am rising above some of the trials and tribulations that life has thrown my way since childhood. Talk about a past of dysfunction—I've been there. There are worse cases, and there are better cases, of growing up, and mine probably is somewhere in the middle. One thing I have always known how to do is make the best of difficult situations, and to be thankful for good things. My Scottish stubbornness and a sense of independence have also served me well.

I was conceived, un-planned, during a college beach trip. My parents eloped, separated within one year, and divorced, before I had a chance to know my father, Leonard. He went on to marry his high school sweetheart, and he developed a great career in radio and television. My mother, Sherry, went on to practice alcoholism, had a nervous breakdown, and spent a couple of short stints in dry out clinics of some sort.

I believe she never actually admitted that she was an alcoholic, saying she was a "problem drinker" and never completely quit; her lengthy binges came and went throughout my life. Her attempts at suicide, at least two that I know of, did not work out.

After the divorce, Sherry, my mother, and I went to live with her parents in Barboursville, West "By God" Virginia. My grandfather was a doctor, a general practitioner, who started his practice during the depression, and was paid in meat, eggs, honey, and maybe moonshine in those early days. He was a workaholic who seemed to love his work and his patients, although he also needed some distance from his nagging wife.

Feeling stifled at home, Sherry was unhappy in a small town with nothing to do, and felt that her parents were watching everything she did. So she decided to move us to Ft. Lauderdale when I was about two, taking a job as a high school English teacher. We enjoyed being near the ocean, and I loved jumping over the waves at the beach. We had a nice two story apartment in a complex with a swimming pool, but I enjoyed toddling away from home for a swim after a hard week at kindergarten. Some pictures of Sherry and Ed were on a bookshelf, and I wanted to know my father. One vivid memory was of our coat closet; below the stairway, dark and empty. When I opened it, my eyes and nose immediately burned with what must have been eau de mildew. This was the early 1960s and maybe air conditioners and dehumidifiers were not as effective then. My favorite TV show was "Captain Kangaroo," and I was often still in my PJs eating cereal with Mr. Green Jeans, when it was time to leave for kindergarten. The teacher had told mother that sending me in my PJs a few times should correct the problem, but she never did that.

On one memorable evening, I guess that my pouting threats to go live with Mimi and Grand-daddy were put to the test, because mother took me out to the sidewalk, a suitcase in hand, and said she'd called a cab to take me to West Virginia! I suspect that my gut reaction was probably traumatic, because I still do not remember what happened next, although it was certainly not a cab ride. A three-year old boy probably wouldn't have had the cash for such a trip. During this time, Sherry's drinking binges probably began in earnest, although I don't remember any of it. It's funny how alcohol can affect one's memory, even if you don't drink.

My grandmother told me that she and Grand-Daddy visited us, and discovered Sherry was having drinking binges on the weekends. She was asked to resign after her second year of teaching, for being drunk on the job. Thus, we moved back to West Virginia, and I began pre-school. I was always reminded to be a nice boy. This is a variation on the old "speak when spoken to" school of child rearing. Even during childhood, I was incensed by this apparent usurpation of my own authority, since it seemed to stifle my self expression and natural curiosity.

By elementary school, I had frequent problems with time management, understanding verbal directions, and forgetfulness. When my report card said "doesn't manage time effectively," how the heck was I, a first grader, to know what that was? Even though I seemed a bright, nice boy, the teachers reminded me to put on my pretend thinking cap, in hopes I could pay attention during class. Otherwise, I tended to daydream, or 'gather wool' as one teacher reported it. Boredom may have set in, but I was always reading above grade level and excelled on spelling tests. How could such a bright young man also forget to do his homework, and be so incompetent at math? Perhaps I was just lazy, and I was constantly reminded to just "apply myself."

I have since decided it was difficult to reach my potential with un-diagnosed ADHD, and being a nice person has not always helped get any of my own needs met. Being a nice boy, or man, is not all it is cracked up to be.

Charles Myers is a creative tinkerer and a jack of many trades. He has lived in Maryland since high school, and works as a computer professional at UMBC. He likes to live and learn, to enjoy variety in all of life's endeavors, and questions conventional wisdom whenever possible. He is interested in current events, Belgian Ale, and photography and he has been a member of the Creative Alliance for more than ten years. His recent publication, "Light Travels," is a 2007 photo calendar and is available at www. lulu.com/cemyers77. He has always wanted to write about some of his early experiences, to share and perhaps help others; the "Write Here, Write Now" nonfiction worksop was a starting point.

Single-Mom Buzzard

Eugenie Nable

I saw the buzzard across the clearing, hunched and stepping forward, away from the sway-back hay crib set at the edge of the woods. The bird was a young adult— its head shiny jet-black, and its feathers smooth and oiled, not tattered or dull. It must have been inside the shed when it heard my car crunching down the drive, and ducked out through a torn board near the ground. At about thirty feet from the shed, eyes on my car, then on me when I got out, the dark creature stopped still to be unseen, one leg raised mid-air, watching to see if I would approach. I walked backwards towards the house so I could see the buzzard and then stood quietly. Seeing that I was father away, the bird lowered the raised leg, then pivoted ninety degrees and loped through a low-grass area. It hopped three times, stretched its wings, pushed onto the air, and landed on the branch of a nearby White Oak, where it perched like a sentry.

You beautiful buzzard! There weren't too many people who would agree with my take on sighting the primitive creature. My thirty-five-year-old godson would agree, and most likely he had already encountered the creature while looking at the old house behind me that he and his wife were moving into today. My husband would also agree with me. He's always admired buzzards and takes the time to watch them as much as he watches a hawk or a heron.

I turned around toward the red-roofed farmhouse

and marveled that this place still existed, hidden from the road by other houses and woods and surrounded by ten acres of pasture and about thirty more acres of woods. Historic Ellicott City was about a mile east of the area. The current owners had bought the land and house from the Rogers family in the early eighties and lived there for twenty two years, upgrading and maintaining the character of the house, even exposing and preserving the 18th-century wattle-and-daub bones of the original structure in one of the hallways and front entrance. Now they had it on the market, renting until they got their price from the right developer.

The outbuildings ranged from old to falling apart; the oldest and farthest away was the hay crib from which the buzzard had emerged. Since no one else had arrived yet with the household items, I headed up the hill to explore the nearest building, which was also the newest, made of concrete blocks covered with stucco, circa 1950. The structure was a small double stable, separated by a four foot high wall and a metal gate—the stable probably once housed goats or ponies. Three other sheds held small farming and gardening equipment, broken wicker chairs, a row boat and a kayak, and lots of crusty stuff that I instantly coveted.

My godson had found this place for rent on Craigslist, and when he met with the owner at the house, Aaron convinced him not to wait on the people who had come first and wanted to rent the house by presenting the owner with a credit report that showed he was a good risk, that he would pay on time and in full. With his foresight, quick thinking, and good luck, he had signed the lease within an hour of meeting with the owner.

What a score—people had lived here since the original part of the house was built around 1760 by the Rogers family—so much history in the house and perhaps even artifacts in any remaining kitchen middens or other refuse sites long buried in the earth. And now that I saw there was a buzzard nesting on the grounds, I clearly felt a gentle envy, braided with longing and excitement.

This place was perfect for Aaron and Michelle, a North Florida man and an East Tennessee woman, both more at ease as Peace Corps volunteers in Uzbekistan than as commuters living in Baltimore. As I mused about their new digs, a truck pulling a long-bed trailer filled with their household belongings slowly crunched its way down the driveway and stopped next to the house. They had extracted their oversized couch and chair from the second floor window of their apartment on St. Paul Street, using a shop sign and an iron grate below the window to loop and anchor the rope, hoist and lower the plush giants down to the street. One year of city living had been enough for them; too much noise, too much hassle having a large dog not used to concrete, too hard to park, and too many mice in the kitchen.

Mice were sure to have taken up residence in this house, too, though they'd be a different variety—perhaps field mice. New sections had been added on to the house throughout the last two centuries, creating freshly cleared ground and open structures, so there was probably a vast tribe of rodent clans descended from the first pregnant mouse that had moved in with the Rogers family as they built their homestead. I was sure the buzzard clan had been there quite a while, too, returning each generation to the familiar nesting grounds.

As we unloaded and schlepped boxes and rugs and lamps, I asked Aaron about the buzzard and he told me that he had seen it by the hay crib the first time he drove out to meet with the landlord. The day after he had signed the lease, he came out to clear a shed to store some items and looked in each structure to see what was there and saw two eggs out in the hay crib. He left quickly because he didn't want to leave his smell or disturb them.

"Two eggs?" I was excited. "Have you seen the mother again?"

"Yeah, she had a fish tail yesterday when I came out to drop off some stuff."

"Aaron, this is awesome...this house with all this land, and an actual buzzard nest. Steve just got a new camera—we'll come out after work to take some photos. We'll be really careful and not disturb the nest when we come. Hope Mamma Bird won't be around." *A nest—a real buzzard nest, I've never seen a buzzard nest....*

Aaron hollered at one of his work buddies getting out of his Jeep to help with the moving. I could tell Aaron was really happy to be out of the city.

I looked up into the tree and the buzzard was gone. Then I saw her still as a rock back on the ground near the crib, watching all the commotion near the house. No one had lived in the house for six months, so it must have been an island of quiet safety for the buzzard, and for other wildlife nearby. Now the noise and presence of humans might drive her away, but where would she find another place to nest?

As an adult, I hadn't really thought much about buzzards, although one morning last winter, I spotted a group of twenty or so perched on a water tower and thought they were clever to use the tower. And recently, an acquaintance described buzzards that roosted each sundown on their newly-built house, how they landed with a thump on the roof, clomped their way to the balconies to sleep, and upon waking, pooped onto decks and plate glass windows as they pushed off into the morning sky.

Observing the poised bird across the way, I laughed, remembering childhood encounters with the critters and how my friends and I tempted buzzards when we were kids. We were a bunch—brothers Chet and Ripper, sisters Cookie and Lulu, and other friends Arden, Bitsy, Big Bill and Little Bill, Wanda Jean, T-Bone, and my brother Mike. On Saturdays, after we did our chores, our small tribe often took off together to wander the fields and woods. Sometimes we trooped barefoot far into a cow pasture to find a clean and open spot so we could lie flat on the ground and play dead, heads toward the center of a circle with tanned arms and legs radiating out toward a staggered circumference. With plenty of space between us, we pretended to be corpses to attract the buzzards down to us.

To get them to come close, and even land to check you out, you had to be still, really still, even if a deer fly landed on you. You could barely breathe as you peered through your fingers to protect your eyes. You'd keep your head stiff and slip your eyes sideways to watch as ten or twenty buzzards landed on those chicken feet and cautiously trod around our bodies. The buzzards appeared to arrive all at once, silent except for a few grunts and the syncopated thuds they made as each one landed. Only the black-headed ones got really close to you on the ground; the red-skinned ones flew over us but never landed. If we didn't scare them off by giggling or squealing, you could get them to come right up to you.

Ripper swore that one pecked his head, but no one saw it happen.

As the big birds plodded up to you, it was just too much to bear. I saw a buzzard come really close to Arden and eyeball his toes, so he was the first to chicken out. He hollered and waved his arms to make the buzzard back off and jump straight up, so startled that it hissed and hopped off, loping a few bounds for lift-off, provoking the departure of the others.

One of the buzzards puked on Chet when it couldn't get away fast enough.

Now *that* was fun.

Go figure... These buzzard memories have just been sitting here in my head all these years! And here in Ellicott City, a half century later, is another buzzard close enough for me to see its heavy legs lumber down the short runway for takeoff. Noises from unloading the truck must have startled it into leaving the nest area again.

That night after I got home, I turned on my laptop and Googled "buzzard," then clicked on a link to the International Turkey Vulture Society. I learned that buzzards are actually North American vultures, and are two distinct species. The correct name for the big brown, red-headed one is "turkey vulture" and the name for the all black one is "black vulture." Both are bald so that when they poke their heads into a dead animal's guts for feasting, the decaying flesh and entrails will not stick to any head or neck feathers. They clean their heads and beaks by baking in the sun, which dries any blood or bodily detritus and also radiates bacteria to death.

Their legs are also featherless for the same reason. Nature has provided them with a powerful cloaca that generates pure uric acid in their anti-microbial excrement: they pee and poop on their legs to kill any bacteria, and they also do the same for their eggs and nest area. When I got close to them during my childhood forays, I expected them to stink, but they did not smell so bad after all, though I recall a definite olfactory disturbance. Since they prefer to eat dead herbivores rather than dead carnivores, and because they eat greens that grow near water or in water such as hyacinths, pickerel, and dollar weed, and also discarded pumpkins, they don't have that acrid, gaggy-sweet musk of heavy meat eaters.

On the International Turkey Vulture Society website, close-up photos show three adult black vultures hanging out with two red-wattled turkey vultures on a wooden fence near a small barn. Though they don't interbreed, they must recognize they are kin, since they help each other discover carrion. In terms of species evolution, the turkey vulture is an older, New World vulture, while the black vulture developed later. The black vulture finds carrion or small animals mostly by sight, while the turkey vulture has a highly developed sense of smell, along with good sight. Now I understood why red-head buzzards rarely landed with the others when we played dead in the cow pasture. They could smell that we were *not* decaying, and therefore not soft enough to peck at and pull apart with their weak beaks. They use their chicken feet only to hold down carrion, not to grasp or tear the body. They appear to have *bird toes*, just barely what you would call talons. Vultures cannot tear open the tough hides of large, newly-dead animals such as deer or wild pigs, which we may have resembled because of our size.

Often, the black vulture will follow the turkey vulture on its rounds because of its superior olfactory awareness. The turkey vulture is the shark of the skies because like a bottom-feeding shark, it can smell a micro whiff of blood or broken flesh miles from its origin. What they so acutely smell is a gas called *mercaptan*, produced by the beginnings of decay. The turkey vulture also benefits when gregarious black buzzards sight a distant potential meal. If the animal is large, they gather in the sky until they have enough vultures to eat the carrion efficiently—perhaps there's also safety in numbers from predators.

It's strange to me now that I wasn't the least bit curious to actually learn about buzzards when I was a kid. They were ubiquitous creatures that carried out their clean-up services on the highways and in the fields, and I just took them for granted. But then I tell myself that ornithologists probably didn't have that much information in the fifties about these creatures, anyway. Maybe.

On the Vulture Society website, I also learned that these primitive birds pair-bond for life and take turns tending the nest. But at the hay crib, there was only one adult that tended the two eggs, and later the chicks, so I assumed the Ellicott City black vulture was a single mom. In the months to follow, we only saw the one adult flying up into the sky, decoying a potential predator away from the nest.

Just before sundown one evening, when we ventured to look into the hay crib to take photos, there was only one adult in the nest. I worried about the eggs. *What if she can't keep them warm enough because she's busy getting food? She looks awfully skinny.* Perhaps her mate was killed by a car as it tried to retrieve a dead animal from the side of the road; this happens often. Even though they are a federally protected species, they can't protect themselves from cars. When they land to eat road kill, they gorge themselves and become too heavy for lift off, unless they disgorge their load first. That's how they get killed by cars—they just can't get out of the way in time.

In April, I wrote Ramona VanRiper, President of the International Turkey Vulture Society, and asked a lot of questions about the nesting buzzard. Ms. VanRiper answered many of my questions, including why these giants in the bird world have no song or squawk, because I wondered if they even had vocal cords, since I had never heard them cry as hawks do. In my early encounters with them, they had never cried out as a gull or a blue jay does. I told her that I knew they hiss and retch with a dry heave or with actual vomit, and that they make gurgling stomach sounds, a prequel to the barfing, but I had never heard a cry. She explained that vultures do not cry out in warning or call to attract mates and postulates; that because they are not predators, they do not need a clarion call to terrorize and flush out prey.

One afternoon in June, my husband and I decided to check on the eggs and photograph them. As we approached the little shed, we both saw that one of the eggs had hatched. A baby buzzard, like a little statue, stood next to the remaining egg. Steve took some photos and we withdrew quickly. I dropped a dead bird that my cat had killed near the nest and we left. As we walked back to visit with my godson, we saw the mother bird up on her safe perch in the big oak. She had probably seen us coming and flew up into the tree before we reached the shed.

After receiving the photo of the brown-splotched vulture eggs and newly-hatched chick, all tan fuzz and black head and not particularly cute, Ms. VanRiper wrote me back to say that the chick was about three days old. She also informed me that it was important that I not leave any food inside the nest or too near because foxes or other predators would be attracted by the smell and might also kill and eat the chicks. I worried that the mother buzzard wasn't getting enough food since she was a widow and had to raise the chicks all by herself, so every bird, squirrel, mouse, or rat that my cats killed and dragged to the door, ended up on the woodpile about fifty feet away from the hay-crib nest.

Each time I visited, the mother would perch in her tree and watch me as I walked down the grassy path to bring her another meal. By then, I had begun to collect fish heads from the seafood shop, and scraps the butcher at the grocery store would give me. Then one morning during rush hour, driving to work on Ritchie Highway near Annapolis, I spotted a freshly-hit possum. *No, don't even think about it! Keep going.* But, further down the road, I spotted a dead raccoon, and knew I had to do it. I braked as soon as I could and turned the car around to retrieve these new-found meals for the single-mom buzzard. The possum and the coon had been hit the night before or early that morning. I had just learned that vultures actually prefer recently deceased carcasses rather than rank and rotting ones, so these would be perfectly ripe by the time I delivered them that evening to Ellicott City. Fortunately, I had a cooler in the trunk I used for cold grocery items, and plastic bags I could use as hand covers while picking up the dead critters.

The traffic on Ritchie Highway during morning rush hour is dense, and I pulled off the road and bumped along the shoulder until I saw the dead possum up ahead. I stopped the car, turned the key, and popped the trunk, stepping out cautiously as the cars whizzed by. With cool efficiency, in stockings and high heels, I strode to the trunk, reached in and pulled out plastic bags, then opened the cooler to make it ready for deposit. I covered my hands, each with a plastic bag, took a deep breath, and walked crisply over to the possum, half squashed, mouth open and sharp little teeth showing, so white and perfect.

I could tell the possum was an adolescent because its coat was a light grey, extremely clean and feathery, not dark grey, dirty and greased down as they can look when they're near the end of their life span, which is about six years. This little guy was only about a year old—still pink and pretty. As I maneuvered the possum body to unstick it from a bloody spot, and smelled the gore, I felt like I was going to hurl, for sure. I can barely clean up cat puke without gagging and sometimes even vomiting, so this was a real challenge, but I had to do it for the single-mom buzzard. I held the possum's head and as quickly as I could, I pulled the bag over the body with my other hand, then when it was pretty much inside, I tied it and slipped the other bag over the bundle and tied the second bag. Then I stepped away and panted, focusing on some small blue wildflowers. I took a long breath, picked up the bagged possum and plunked it in the cooler.

As I got back in the car to drive another mile to find the raccoon, I realized the second retrieval would be more public. The possum had been on the right side of the road, near bushes and trees, and with my car parked behind it, passing cars couldn't see much of what I was up to. The raccoon, on the other hand, was at the edge of the median visible at the divide to cars passing on both sides of the highway.

Well, so what. The coon is at the side of a short turn lane that no one in their right mind would try and use at this time of day. I have to do this. She needs some help to survive. OK. Yes, I'm in my right mind. Pull over slowly. There it is. Breathe. Just act matter-of-fact, casual. Here goes...

Setting my face with a neutral, not-quite-mindless expression, I went about the business of packing up the second road kill in the same way I had collected the possum. The raccoon was bigger and more unwieldy, and of course, this had to be one of the few days I wore heels and a skirt, so not only did I have to bend one knee down to the ground, reach over with my plastic bag mittens and scoop up the dead one, and wrap it up with my arms extended so I wouldn't get any guts on my clothes, I also had to look graceful and pleasant as I carried out the retrieval. I tried not to notice people in their cars staring at me as I wrestled with the brushy striped tail to stuff it into the bag, and failed, because it kept popping back out, blown and flipped by the traffic's wake.

But I could feel the gawks and disbelieving stares and could see some laughing, and some totally grossed out expressions out of the corner of my eye. *Get this done...Yes, officer, I am an official road kill inspector, so now if you'll just excuse me, I've got to get this baby to the lab...* As I stood and rushed the body into the cooler, I lost all my contrived demeanor and began to retch and gag. I sprang to the front of my car and bent forward thinking that now I would really lose my cookies, but I only blasted a couple of dry heaves with just a little reflux. Yuck. I stood back up only to begin gagging again—this time from car exhaust, carbon dioxide and monoxide fumes. I breathed through my jacket and strolled to the back of my car and gently closed the cooler, then the trunk. The delivery wagon was loaded and ready to travel the route to the distant woodpile, where the road kill offerings would be placed with great reverence and retching.

Later that month, Steve photograph the buzzard babies for the last time. I asked him to stop taking photos of them, because after each shoot, the mother buzzard would move the nest further into the hay crib. The first time she moved the eggs; the second time she moved the one chick and egg; and the third time after Steve took snaps of the two chicks, I'm sure she moved them again. I thought she was getting freaked out and expending way too much energy protecting her chicks from the human bringing in the lightning to the nest. I wrote another letter to Ramona VanRiper, which she never answered, not because she thought I was crazy or weird, because *she* carries Tupperware containers in her trunk for her roadkill collection, but perhaps because we disturbed the chicks and mother by photographing them, or because I still called the creatures buzzards and not vultures. Who knows? I included the photos:

Hello Ramona,

Steve took one more set of photos of the buzzard babies, while their single-parent mom was out foraging. He said they froze like little statues. You can see that one has its wing extended and it stayed like that for three photos—one photo was flash. They seem to have a buzzard language, even though they don't vocalize. Those eyes are ancient and surely see the memory of their kind.

I place cat kill (bird remains, rats, mice, a regurgitated squirrel, and sometimes cut-up chicken from the grocery store) on a woodpile located a good ways from the shed. She watches us from her branch up in a nearby tree and flies down to get her snack when we are far enough away.

I wonder if her mate got hit by a car early on. Assume she will get another mate after her offspring fly the coop to roost with other adults. I would guess that each generation returns to their birth nest. It seems logical that one would come back to nest in the hay crib for as long as it remains there—though development is on the horizon.

Is there a design for a vulture house that could be placed in protected areas? I've seen wood duck boxes and bluebird boxes promoted by state and federal agencies. Is there a Vulture House program? They certainly need more space for nesting quarters... As they navigate thermal updrafts miles up in the sky, would they recognize a nest house made just for them?

I will always remember the clean, sharp smell of the nest in the hay crib, the brown-spotted eggs resting on the floorboard splashed with dried excrement. Who would have thought that uric acid in the droppings purifies, kills bacteria?

Enjoy the photos and save for your archives. I have come to admire and cherish these beautiful buzzards.

Sincerely,

Eugenie VanHoten Nable

Eugenie V. Nable, M.A., has worked in the non-profit sector, state government, college/university, and for private researchers as an abstractor, educator, and editor/writer.

She has researched, written, and edited content for public information, training, and education materials regarding federal and state legislation, student financial assistance, English as a Second Language, state arts programs, medical and health concerns, and most recently, sexual violence and women's issues.

Our Last Night Together

Holly Myers

Tonight would be the last night I would sleep with his unclaimed shirts surrounding me. I loved his personal scent. It was a blend of fabric softener and male sophistication. It had taken two months, but my mind now had my heart thinking that maybe, just maybe, it was the scent that I missed more than the man. Did I really love him? Was he really funny and clever? Or was he merely another relationship that started off at that level of perfection that, when the spark fizzles, your memory of the perfection keeps you together months longer than necessary?

Decidedly, he had to go. So long as that stupid alluring scent was around so, too, would be my desire to have him back. Cut them? Throw them away? No. He didn't deserve that. I would wash his memory away that following morning. I would pack up his shirts and miscellaneous items that lingered in my house, haunting me. I'd done the right thing. It was time to move on. Move into acceptance of my choice. Move into anger at his flaws; if that's what it would take.

Did I do the right thing? I miss him.

That night I cuddled up next to him. There was little fragrance left. I turned the shirts inside out, sniffing like a hound to track remaining pieces of him.

I don't have to wash the shirts. I can keep him with me as long as I want. Relax. Go to sleep.

I inhaled my way back into our life together. I let

the good thoughts flood in, breathing in every good memory that, after tonight, I would erase. He enjoyed absurd stories and rants as well as I. Our favorite pointless raving was about the ignorance of panda bears.

"Why should people step in to prevent their dying off? Any species too dumb to know how to mate should abstain its way into extinction," he would say so resolutely.

And my heart delighted in the little favors: brushing my long, tangly hair, drawing my bubble bath and lighting crisp linen-scented candles, nightly setting the coffee pot's timer to begin brewing as I was getting ready for work.

He stopped being attentive. His doting gestures faded. Selfless favors did not come naturally to him.

No one else held the same passion for raw fish. At least once a week we would go out to dinner at Kiku's Sushi. We were such regular customers that the owner and chef began giving us free food. Smiling over steamed edamame, he would tickle my knee from under the table in a booth or scootch my stool in towards him at the bar. We shared the love of food in general. He never commented that I'd eaten a lot, or that I never seemed to get full.

He had nothing nice to say about anyone. Even his own friends could "use more muscle tone," or "hit the gym more frequently." What did he really think about my body?

Cooking was a delight, not a chore. We listened to bluegrass while julienning and sautéing. In the warmer months we liked to have the windows open, allowing fresh air to invigorate us during the food preparation. Everything was done with care. Each knife stroke had a proper technique that he taught me. He cheered me as I zested my first lemon. We were like a circus act commanding control over serrated edges while two-stepping around a kitchenette. If our cooking was precise, our conversation was happy-go-lucky. All we wanted was the time to talk, mindlessly chatter about nothing. Rarely did we contaminate the kitchen with an issue more momentous than the comeback of eighties punk rock fashion.

He changed. Or did he? Had he always been full of himself? Remember that time he barked, "Is that how I taught you to zest a lemon?" Forget about him. Just go to sleep. He will be gone in the morning.

We sure could entertain friends. We hosted Thursday night potluck dinners. He would send an email in which he divulged the highly anticipated theme to the group—stir fry night, taco night, fondue night, casserole night, finger foods night. They all came and went with great fanfare. I loved his obsession for having prep work out of the way before people came. We would have a few spare minutes of quiet to share a drink before the pack arrived; time to snicker about who would show up with a lackluster dish or who would be distasteful enough to pass off something from the Whole Foods hot bar. As everyone milled around we would cozy into the other's neck, or whisper catty comments about our guests to each other. Was our bond formed from touting ourselves as the greatest people who ever lived? At other people's expense?

He was just insecure. There were things he could not express. He wanted to. Deep down he was compassionate. He even volunteered at a GED class on his Tuesday nights.

What difference did it make? I had to move forward. Tomorrow I would push back the blue and black geometric-print sheets, his favorite, and truly begin without him. I'd grieved, I'd cried, I'd yelled, I'd drunk, I'd eaten, I'd shopped. That's what was done, and then they were gone. I rolled into his shirts, snuggling into them and his side of the bed. I took one long, belly breath. His smell was so apparent I could feel him beside me. His smooth, toned skin. His toes that I liked to weave my toes between. His calves that bulged from his constant bike riding. His ear lobe that my fingers would trace as we fell asleep. I could feel it all. I could even feel my scalp tingle as he strung his fingers through my hair.

He never stopped that. He always tousled my hair. Why couldn't I have waited for him to come back around? Why did I have to be heading for the door to get him to express how he felt? What if I just go back and explain that I felt unloved and neglected. He'd be so relieved to have our mix-up resolved.

Crying into his shirts, I took another long breath. I coughed from such a deep breath. Too fatigued to analyze or hypothesize anymore, I pressed his maroon v-neck to my cheek. This time I took my final lungful of him, expanding my rib cage to capacity, making sure to inhale every last scent from the fibers. Keeping my hands clasped around both of his shirts, I fell asleep.

At the alarm, I popped out of bed. The shirts had knotted themselves around my arms like two necklaces thrown haphazardly into a jewelry box. Gently, I untied them and went to the washing machine. I started the water. I measured out the soap. I poured the detergent into the machine. I waited for the water and soap to mix. I let the water fill the machine.

There is a better life waiting for you. There is. You can do this. It's right to do this.

I plunged my hands into the soapy water, kneading both shirts until they were soaked. I threw my geometric print sheets on top. I looked into the washer, watched the shirts and sheets swirl. I dropped the lid down, latching the washer door shut.

Holly Myers is a teacher in Baltimore. Prior to taking a creative turn, her nonfiction appeared in The Journal of Homeland Security *and* The Washington Times. *About "Our Last Night Together" Holly says, "I wrote this piece during a break-up from the one who I hoped would be the final one. Fortunately for me he wasn't or I would have missed out on the love of my life."*

Ruth's Chris: A Review

Nicole Walton

Ruth's Chris has a new place outside Ocean City, Maryland. Store No. 95, the waiter would tell us. And that Stores 1 through 94, with their identical menus, are just as nice. The enterprise went public this year.

Peering in through the front window, it's like a deluxe paddock in there, or maybe a ski lodge, with a loft and an open floor plan. Let's go with *paddock*, because *ski lodge* implies mountain, and there's no mountain here. It's as flat as a cow patty around here, except for the manufactured lumps of roughened turf that stud the golf course we just passed, the one made of excavated rubble. There's new housing next to it. Beyond that is some remaindered forest and a second, wooded course, with some of its greens running into marshland. Turning in from Route 50, across from the Home Depot and the Wal-Mart, the project resembles an enormous litter box. Picture acres of soiled sand, overturned by monstrous feral cats. Beyond it all, along the muddy tidal marshlands, which flank the Isle of Wight Bay, the winding ribbon of fresh black asphalt, has threaded us through various phases of housing development, until at last we've found ourselves at the club. So *this* is Ruth's Chris.

We wait for our table in a long hallway, seated on high, medieval-looking chairs that make us all feel like children because our feet do not quite touch the ground.

Out front, an impossibly long stretch limo pulls up. The limo is black and has decorative red and yellow flames air brushed down the side of it. Some people emerge, wearing laminated nametags and matching polo shirts. They are escorted immediately to somewhere we cannot see. A secret room! They must be special. The limo slinks away. Shortly thereafter, we three—my father, my daughter, and I—are escorted into the main dining area of the restaurant.

Our waiter is knowledgeable about the menu. With the cheerful persuasive skills of a man who most likely sells time shares (to married couples only!) in rural Virginia during the day, he tells us with great care about the enormous lumps of corn-fed beef that we can purchase, *a la carte*, along with large platters of *a la carte* mashed potatoes, potatoes which sit in about a half a pound of melted garlic butter. *Mmmm.* And, we can start with the much-touted, *signature a la carte chop salad,* which, when it arrives, has a vertical structure and as far as we can tell, is comprised entirely of shredded romaine lettuce and mayonnaise, with a chiffonade of cooled french-fried onions on top.

My father has an $80 gift card to spend, a gift from his eigthieth birthday. It buys us two of those luscious *a la carte* steaks, oh boy! We choose petit filets, the smallest on the menu. When they arrive, we realize we should've split one between us. My father and I receive our enormous lumps of brightly red meat, seared on the outside to absolute perfection. There is nothing else on our large, white plates. From the outset, it is clear we can't possibly eat it all, but the bits we are able to eat practically melt in our mouths. My daughter, ten years old, receives the boned chicken, a whole *poussin* with all of the bones removed except for its cute little drumsticks, and it comes wrapped around about ten ounces of imitation Boursin "cheese." Our meat is delivered to us on plates we are told are *five hundred degrees so don't touch them!* To be fair our server then makes a big deal about transferring my daughter's chicken to a cooler plate without even being asked to do so, but I suspect he is engaging in a bit of performance art on behalf of his tip.

I confess to you that we are here under false pretenses. My father made the reservation under the name *Jones*, because he is good and tired of having to spell *Schultheis* every time he calls someone on the phone who wants to write down his old world name. This results in our being called *Mr.* and *Mrs.* and *Miss Jones* repeatedly. My daughter is asking, "Why do they keep calling us *Jones*?" and "Why do they have to call us anything?" and "Bob-Bob, why didn't you just say *Bob* if you didn't want to spell *Schultheis*?" and the unanswerable, "What are you going to do when the check comes and you are trying to pay the bill with a credit card with the name of this guy *Schultheis* on it?"

The *Mrs. Jones* part is funny. I guess we make an interesting couple, Dad and me. At eighty-one, he is nearly deaf, has a full set of uppers, and suffers from neuropathy, which makes cutting food difficult for him at times. In addition, his shape is like a football and he walks like Frankenstein. I am thirty years younger, but I have a touch of arthritis and my unfortunate resemblance to him is obvious. Once I was Rosie the Riveter for Halloween. At the Wal-Mart men's department, the blue Dickies that fit me were precisely my father's size.

However, I digress. I am enjoying a fine meal in a fine restaurant, precisely the wrong time to consider one's girth. Anyway, I should be listening to my father, who is telling us about this fine new golf community. He used to work in real estate. Real estate finance, to be precise. And he knows more than I do about our location.

Although we are in a development called *Glen Riddle*, it's not really a *glen*. A glen is a narrow, secluded valley, as in the mountains. Dad explains, because he knows all of this personally, "It's named after the guy who used to own the place. They trained famous race horses here." Actually, the owner was *Sam* Riddle, a textile magnate from Pennsylvania, and he named the place after the hometown his grandfather founded. This before that was a famous old name in Scotland that had to do with winnowing wheat and rye. Now the famous paddock is a steakhouse. Much of the original structure was used in the design. Therefore, there are these lovely touches, like old stall doors that have been polished and made into tables in the bar.

If you buy one of the $600,000-plus Glen Riddle Fairway houses, constructed by Centex Corporation (a Dallas-based builder with assets exceeding $21 billion), you can choose from two popular models, the *Man O'War* and the *War Admiral*. Don't worry if you can't qualify for a bank mortgage, because Centex provides financing, too! And don't forget Centex's HomeTeam Pest Defense. Should any undesirable vermin invade, these cement slab houses are designed with a masterful built-in system of portals and vents that facilitate extermination without agents ever having to enter the home. There is something vaguely troubling about all of this, but I can't put my finger on it.

Unfortunately, we haven't met any of the people who live in these warring houses with their built-in defense systems, nor are we likely ever to meet them, since we don't play golf. But at dinner, they seem nice. In fact, my daughter is so impressed with their grooming, she says to me at one point, "Mom, why do all of the women look like they come from soap operas?" I can't answer her, but she's right. There are many shellacked blonde-haired women with perfect makeup in here. Tall. Skinny blue jeans and high-heeled boots. Tinted eyeglasses with jewels on them, manicured fingers with designs on them, and sculpted fur jackets.

Towards the end of our meal, we notice that many men are wearing athletic shoes and tailored leather jackets. When they drape their jackets over the backs of their chairs, you see they are wearing beepers or cell phones and sometimes both on their waists while they eat. Truly, we don't belong to any country clubs, and with the name *Schultheis* my parents were never asked to join one when I was a kid, but now I know what you are supposed to wear.

Suddenly I feel a presence at my ear. For a moment, I think it is the waiter, but no, it is a whisper from my husband. He is not with us tonight, but he is asking me a question nonetheless. "Are all the faces white in there?" I look around. "Yes," I whisper back. "Except for the waiter at the table behind us." The loquacious fellow smiles widely across his large, perfect teeth while explaining to the diners behind us, with a flourish of white-linened forearm, the origins of *Ruth's Chris*. One of the diners says something in reply that is meant to be amusing, and the waiter dutifully laughs.

"What did you say?" my father asks. I had turned back around, and was moving my lips.

"Nothing. Just talking to myself."

"What?"

Ah. He's turned off his hearing aids. They drive him crazy, cutting in and out, when in a noisy place.

When the check arrives, we're given a gargantuan plastic shopping bag with handles. The bag sports the famous *Ruth's Chris* logo. It seems vaguely reminiscent of something ominous—what could it be? —with its colors of black, red and white. Inside are our twinned, unfinished hunks of meat. Before being placed in the bag, our precious bovine cargo has been carefully wrapped, separately, in generously sized, black polystyrene clamshells.

As we prepare to leave, I notice a young woman in the unheated carport. She has long chestnut hair and sinewy, muscular legs, which are bare, although it's about 38 degrees at this point. A dark, late fall evening. She has a bit of a belly and is wearing one of those miniscule lacy black acetate slips, with a black push up bra underneath. The bra straps are just a bit shorter than the spaghetti straps on the dress, forcing observers to pause and consider the flesh underneath. Focusing on the legs again, I also note this dress could not possibly be any shorter. On the gamine's feet are enormous black platform shoes with heels higher than anything I have ever seen below the beaches of South Jersey. There is, in fact, a term they use for shoes like this in New

Jersey, but we don't use that kind of language on our beach down here. She is whinnying on her cell phone for a long time, swinging her big red forelocks as she shifts from one foot to the other as, alas, she grows cold at the gate.

Overall, we've had a great evening. Having dined at such aesthetic and culinary heights, which have assured us of our lofty social stature, we are in good spirits. Waving a cheerful goodbye to the pretend soldier at the gingerbread gatehouse on our way out, we cruise past the Berlin, Maryland, Wal-Mart and head east towards the comforting neon lights of home, Ocean City. My father's handicap tags are swinging to and fro from our rear view mirror, and in time with them I find myself humming a song, from a movie I cannot quite remember, "Tomorrow belongs to me!"

Nicole Walton lives in Roland Park with her husband, daughter, and cat. Her work has appeared in Brevity, The Vestal Review, *and* The Daily Record. *As a lawyer, she thought she was very important. She did a lot of legal writing, and much of it was published. She used to take herself way too seriously, but now she is happier. She has written a short play and is working on a screenplay and a novel, and has a bunch of short stories that aren't quite there yet, but maybe she is just having trouble letting go of them.*

The Kiss

Richard Crary

The first time she kissed me, I didn't respond. For one thing, she was drunk. For another, we were in the backseat of another boy's car, with him in the front, and I was very conscious of his presence. They'd dated not too long before and he was still into her. But mostly I just didn't know what to do. I sat there while she kissed me, my hand sort of pinned underneath her, wondering what was going on.

It was junior year, sometime after New Year's. She was blonde, with big hair (it was the 80s), pale blue eyes, her father's big nose, a strong, dynamic personality. She was my best friend. This night she'd called me asking if I wanted to go out with them. I did want to hang out with her (I always wanted to hang out with her), but I wasn't into the drinking (I never did get the drinking). So they picked me up, and sure enough, immediately we were in the midst of their weekly quest to find someone who would buy alcohol for teenagers.

Actually, the first kiss I'm talking about wasn't *technically* the first kiss, though I've always thought of it as such. It wasn't even the first kiss that night. In the course of the search for beer, she'd been trying to convince me to drink with them, but I was adamant; I wasn't having any of it. At one point, before getting out of the car at a pit-stop, she'd leaned over from the front seat into the back where I was sitting, and kissed me. She was wearing one of those Coca-Cola rugby shirts that were inexplicably so popular that year, and it billowed out while she leaned into me. The kiss was more than a peck: it was slow and soft, and she was obviously expecting it to be enough to get me to do what she wanted. It wasn't. So when she kissed me later in the night, my first thought was that it was more of the same, but then it felt different, longer

She pulled back, looked at me for a bit, puzzled, then climbed back into the front seat. At this point, it was late, and we all needed to get back home. On the way to my house, she said several times to our lonely driver, "He hates me."

"I don't hate you; don't be stupid."

The next night, I spoke to her on the phone, and I ventured a remark about the kiss.

"What are you talking about?"

"What? You're kidding right? When you kissed me last night?"

"I have no idea what you're talking about...."

"I can't believe you don't remember." I proceeded to describe in painful detail the course the evening took, the little battles, the beer run, the kiss, the ensuing awkwardness....

"Yeah, I know. I remember. I just wanted to hear what you would say about it."

"I see...."

"So why didn't you kiss back?"

"I didn't know what to do." Really, I didn't. How did people know how to kiss? How did they know *when* to kiss? These were great mysteries to me. It seemed to me that everyone else knew, that everyone else was in on some secret that had been held beyond my grasp.

"You know, you just kiss; it comes naturally, doesn't it?"

"I guess not."

"Anyway, whatever, it's no big deal. I just like to kiss, you know? It doesn't mean anything."

"Ok. If you say so...."

The thing was, I may not have responded to her kiss, but somehow I now had a crude vision that the two of us would someday do more than just kiss. The other thing was that I fell in love with her. Hard. But I didn't know what to do about *that*, either. We were constant companions, always studying together, going to the library, to the movies, except that she always had one boyfriend or another, and I became increasingly unable to understand or accept this fact. When she complained about a particular boyfriend, one who wouldn't leave her alone, I entertained violent fantasies in which, coming to her protection, I made my feelings clear. I was aware of my striking lack of originality in this regard.

The other times she kissed me, I can't say I was ready for it—she always caught me by surprise—but I definitely responded. I liked it. I liked it a lot. I tried to maneuver situations so that she would kiss me, but all this did was frustrate me and give me headaches. I never knew why she kissed me at any given moment. And the notion of initiating a kiss myself filled me with abject terror. How was I to know if she'd be receptive? How could I be certain?

She always seemed so sure of herself. She was assertive, popular with many (she was class president), impatient to be an adult. I was more indirect, introspective; outside of my classes I was known by relatively few kids and those who knew me had me pegged as intelligent and funny, yes, but also surly and sarcastic, and I was in no hurry to grow up. She was always dating somebody; I never dated anybody. It never occurred to me that I could. She seemed to know what she wanted and spoke often of her dreams and desires. I had a hard time imagining my life beyond a certain point. I had a hard time imagining my life as something I participated in.

One night we were studying in the kitchen at her parents' house. She stopped for a moment, looked at me, twirled her hair around a finger, and, moving a pencil in the corner of her mouth, said, "We should do it." Yes.

"Ok." Was she serious? "Where? When?"

"I don't know. But we should do it." But we didn't. Not then, not till much later, in a very different part of our lives.

Our friendship became increasingly contentious. We fought all the time, yelled at each other about the stupidest things. I gave her shit about her smoking (I didn't understand why anyone ever smoked) and drinking. I hated the new group of friends she'd started spending time with; I thought they were taking up too much of her time that could be spent with me. I interrogated her about her boyfriends. She would ask me why I didn't like this or that guy, when really I liked *them* just fine, but I didn't understand how she didn't know that I was in love with her. Wasn't it obvious?

We had some fights that were so bad we ended up not speaking for days. Devastating. Unacceptable. Each time we made up, I was that much more certain that I could not be happy without her in my life. Afraid of losing her as a friend, I became even more tentative than before, even less likely to overtly reveal what I was feeling. I tried to hint at things, at larger feelings, get her to say something that I could assent to with confidence. If she told me that she loved me, then I would feel free to admit my feelings. And I figured that if she wasn't saying anything about it, if she wasn't telling me that *she* loved *me*, then she must not feel that way. After all, she was confident, assertive, bold. Wasn't she? And she'd kissed me all those times, hadn't she? I never imagined that she might have been just as confused as I was, that she knew no more about what she was doing, where she was going, than I did.

We talked on the phone every night. School gossip, music, college, random chit-chat. My attempts to say things designed to elicit some declaration from her did not have the desired effect. She may have picked up on what I was trying to say, but instead of admitting how wrong she'd been, instead of admitting that she loved me, too, she asked, "Are you in love with me?"

Yes! Yes, I am! I wanted to shout, but I panicked; I couldn't believe she was asking me this.

"What?!?"

"Are you in love with me?"

Yes, dammit, *yes. Say it. Say it!*

"No." *Sigh.* "No."

"Good."

Good?

"You should never fall in love with me."

We had more than one exchange following this

pattern. Nothing changed except for an increase in tension, an intensification of our unsaid feelings. We made a mess of things. By the last few months of senior year we were fighting more often than not, or at least it seemed that way to us. We never seemed to understand what the other was talking about; every topic was potential ground for disagreement. She seemed depressed; I was unhappy and always angry.

The prom was coming up. I wanted us to go together, and I was working up my courage to ask her. I was going to do it, I told myself. Then one night at my house she announced that some boy had asked her. She wasn't excited about it (he was just a friend she'd known forever), but since no one else had asked her, she'd said she would go with him. I was astonished. There was a moment in which we both seemed to be waiting for me to say that I wanted her to go with me instead. But I didn't say anything. She went home, and I threw my shoe towards my bedroom as hard as I could, splintering the door.

A few weeks later, in May, just two weeks prior to the prom, we were in our political science class. True to form, the class hadn't started yet, though the bell had long since sounded. The teacher sat towards the front of the class, reading his newspaper, while the rest of us chatted amongst ourselves. I was involved in a conversation about Advanced Placement tests. I was in AP Calculus, most of them were in AP English. I was asked why so few of the AP Calculus students were going to be taking the AP test, when all of the English students were taking theirs. I had a theory about this, the details of which escape me now, but it was one of the many idiotic things she and I had disagreed on in recent weeks. I started to give my answer, but she interrupted me.

I spun in my chair and shouted at her: "Fuck you!" Everyone stopped what they were doing and sat there looking stunned. I was right there with them.

She stared at me. "I can't believe you just said that."

Neither could I.

"Well, I did." As if I wanted someone to tell me that I hadn't.

She gathered all of her books and things and stormed out of the room. "I don't have to take this shit." The teacher made a perfunctory attempt to stop her, but she was gone. I overheard one of her friends say, "For two people who are such good friends, they sure fight *a lot.*"

When class was over (could class possibly have begun?), the teacher pulled me aside and said, "I don't know what's going on here, but if you intend to continue any kind of friendship with her, I strongly suggest you find her and apologize."

Apologize. Yes, obviously. But what could I say? I had no idea why I'd said what I'd said; it had just sort of come out, unbidden. That night, I broke down crying with my mom, who persuaded me to try to call her. I did, but it didn't matter. I tried explaining, but I didn't know what exactly I was explaining. We didn't talk for weeks.

Just before graduation, there was the obligatory awards ceremony, and we were the only two recipients of a certain scholarship. We walked up to the stage, all eyes upon us, a slight murmur flitting among our friends; the tension was thick. On stage, we looked at each other. She seemed different. She was wearing a blue dress. She looked beautiful, but distant. Our eyes met briefly, but just briefly, uncertainly, and we returned to our seats.

Later that day, I was in the guidance counselor's office with some other classmates, when someone came in and said that I was wanted in the hall. I went out, and there she was. She seemed older to me, as if she'd already moved on from this place and its problems. She said something nice about how I looked; I told her she looked great and that I missed her. We hugged. She apologized; I apologized. We agreed to let it go, and we spent the rest of the day with each other, killing time with friends in our favorite teacher's back room. High School was basically over.

A few weeks later, after graduation, we met for lunch at a Chinese restaurant. It was an awkward experience; we didn't know how to be with each other anymore. We were both going to college in the fall, to the same college, and we agreed that we still wanted to be friends. We agreed, but there was little joy in it. We were both tired of fighting. The stated decision to agree to remain friends seemed perfunctory, something you do when you've meant so much to each other, but don't really have to see each other much in the future, even while at the same college. It was a big university, a big world.

Richard Crary lives in Baltimore. He loves books, music, his cats, and his wife Aimée. He writes the blog "The Existence Machine" at http://yolacrary.blogspot.com.

Got!

Tracy Byrnes

Oh, honey, you're in for it. That's the truth. I'll tell you. I'll tell you—you with your baby skin, your silky skin, your happy cheeks. I'll tell you because I want you to be prepared. You're going to need a battle face to get through this, you're going to need a hard shell, honey, a *very hard shell.* And you might as well know that now, because this thing—it's coming soon. So soon you'll never have a chance to dread it. The dread will come later, in the never-ending present, as it slowly dawns on you just how much you're going to miss. Please, don't hate me for scaring you; I'm operating on the assumption that you'll prefer, as I do, to know when a bad thing is coming. I know you have no ability yet to understand what I'm talking about when I use the phrase "unparalleled horror of cystic acne." But please, just trust me. This way, you'll have time, however little, to develop strength before you need it. I am you. I am you in the future, and I need, I want, to tell you about your life.

You're eight and on your way to Laurie Baker's boy-girl birthday party. Or, you're fourteen, and about to start your first day of high school. Or, you're seventeen, and it's the morning of your senior prom. It doesn't matter what age you are, you have it. You always have it. You probably always will.

Anyway, there it is—another one. No, excuse me, another *ones.* You never just have the one. That would be so cliché, so like a moment from a bad teen movie. What you've got goes well past typical. What are you going to do about it? It's too late to treat it, and you can't treat it, really, you know that from experience. Acne medications contain one of two active ingredients: salicylic acid, which has exactly zero effect on you, or benzoyl peroxide, which has the effect of turning your entire face red and itchy. The last option is Accutane, the mother of all acne medications, but that's been vetoed by your dermatologist and your mother, on account of it occasionally causing terrible things— birth defects, depression, even suicide. Never mind that the last thing you're going to get, looking like this, is pregnant. Never mind that depression and suicide, it seems to you, are far more likely to be side effects of *not* taking heavy drugs. But you can't expect a non-sufferer to understand that. So you nod, and agree outwardly that yes, it's better to be ugly and ignored and *alive*, and you go to your party, or wherever you're going, and you deal with it.

Faced with the monumental task of accepting what seems to be fate, you learn coping mechanisms. Your mother, in some divinely-bestowed burst of empathy, decides that if you're old enough to have acne, you're old enough to cover it up. She walks you around the cosmetics counter and tests products on you until you're both experts on the strengths and weaknesses of every concealer under the Nordstrom sun. The makeup ladies smile kindly at you, paid beauties who can always afford to be nice. You buy the best of the best products, along with all the pastel-colored accoutrements that, when used together, mean nobody will be able to tell there's anything wrong with you, provided they keep a distance of ten paces. Your morning routine, in middle school, takes longer than Miss America's. You check the retouching box on the order forms for your school pictures, so that when your parents cut up the sheet of wallet-sized portraits and slip them into the Christmas cards, it will appear as though your family, too, has had a year of beautiful progress.

Of course, none of this equals acceptance. No straight-A report card, merit award, or skating medal is ever going to make up for you having to spend every slumber party of your girlhood trying to stay awake later than all the others, so that you could remove your makeup after everyone was asleep. Nor will those successes make up for the mornings, for which you had to bring along your own personal alarm clock, so that you could get up and put your makeup on again before everyone else woke up. Nor will they atone for that bleak day in history when you cried for three hours after some helpful teen magazine informed you that guys say their number one turn-on is great skin. Nor will they erase the memory of the curious child of a perfect stranger, running up to you, wanting to know—*What's wrong with your face? What happened?* "Um," you'll answer. It will be the only possible response.

And that's just the psychological pain. The dirty little secret no one ever lets slip out is that cystic acne doesn't just hurt, it *hurts*. It feels like there are golf balls growing underneath your skin. If you're thinking about it—and you always are—you can actually detect the swirling movement of the crud in your pores. You imagine the particles of puss and gook together beneath the surface, multiplying, festering, dancing the night away. Once in a while, they cook up a really special one. No ordinary breakout, *this* is a mutant cyst from hell, one so large and painful as to make your face appear misshapen. As if that weren't horrible enough, *this* one feels the need to stick around for months. Months! You look in the mirror one morning in September and think, *oh shit*, and the next thing you know it's February and you're thinking, *shit, shit!* It's still there, on your left cheek, still growing. Like some kind of cartoon affliction, it's taking over your whole head, starting to obstruct your vision.

This disease is no brain tumor. It won't kill you. But it does live on your face, which makes it plenty serious. Think about that: it's *on* your *face*—your greeting to the world. Here you're living in a society that believes dewy skin to be a measure of worth, and yours is covered with an inch-thick layer of what amounts to latex paint. And even so, there's no way the paint is successfully hiding those fuchsia-tinted golf balls. You're too far gone for that.

I just want you to know what you're up against.

I can hear you now, crying, squeaking. *How can this be?* I know, I know, and I'm sorry. It will seem on some days like the end of a turn that never really began. But what I didn't tell you before—the real truth—is that none of this horror stacks up against the awe and vigor of life in the world. You won't miss much of what's important. Your face is like anyone's. It can feel cold wind and hot water, and it will see color and get brown in the sunlight, and it can laugh, and it will be touched, and it will crinkle up just the same.

Think of it this way, honey: you've been *got!* Tagged. Chosen. This is your life, the one that didn't have to happen to you, but it did. You were born into this skin and you belong to it like the moon to a crater. The real truth is that it will never matter if you accept it, because it will accept you. It'll take you in when you're just a kid, making sure you never become the perfect girl everyone wants, or wants to be, who changes according to expectation, who eventually buckles under the weight of it. What *that* girl's got is a too-heavy cross. You can't stand up straight, but it's only because you're looking down; she can't stand up at all. *You can look up.* You can choose to look up. Because of what you've got, you'll learn there's power in being invisible or all-too-visible and nothing in between—you'll see what isn't shown to you, hear what isn't said to you, and never once fear truth and exposure as the worst kind of accidents. It will be the ideal experiential makeup of a life spent writing.

So, like I said, prepare. What you've got, what's got you, will change everything. After you've squirmed and wriggled in this skin, after you've thrashed and fought and struggled in this skin, you'll find yourself, someday, standing still—still in the locked embrace of everything you are, but not ugly, not ignored. Alive.

Tracy Byrnes thinks writing turned out to be better for her skin than medication. She lives in Baltimore.

A Gentleman's Garden

Rick Connor

I feel free. I regard downtown and my whole life at
once. I can see over the top of the Basilica to the shore
of Fells Point. I like my new job and my apartment; I've
made some friends, now have a garden, and recently
met Peter. All feels right with the world, especially in
Reservoir Hill.

I'm on Whitelock Street at Linden Avenue, desolate
now, but where thirty years ago thrived a barbershop,
a bakery, and a laundromat. One hundred years before
that stood the majestic homes of Baltimore's most
prominent families. They fled the city for the suburbs in
the sixties, and left behind their unaffordable properties.
Most were sold cheaply to developers who slashed them
up into small units, and rented them to poor families.
Many homes were just abandoned; squatters, drugs, and
violence eventually invaded, slowly ravaged, and now
entirely rule the community.

I'm standing on a mound of saturated earth in the
middle of a bare garden, fenced in. Mr. Montgomery
and I dug up the ground ourselves in the corner of an
empty field. Mr. Montgomery is seventy-something.
He's lived in this neighborhood for over thirty years,
and is well known for rallying his neighbors around
hot topics: crime, sanitation, rat eradication, and now a
community garden. From my plot I have an unobstructed
view down the street to the Res Hill Community Center

where I work. Halfway there, at the corner of Lakeview Avenue, young men operate a prosperous open air drug market. They shoot craps on the broad sidewalk, smoke blunts, lounge on collapsed marble steps. They stash their drugs under fallen porches, and lean against the graffiti-covered walls: *RIP Shorty, Footie, Congo, Furley.* They drink beer, and spit.

I am hoeing a furrow for the lettuces that have already sprouted on my kitchen windowsill when I hear a car and look up to see Peter parking his sleek silver Nissan. Weeks earlier, Peter showed up at the community center and said, "We know what you're trying to do here. The Friends want to help." I was turning a church-run soup kitchen over to the people who ate there, and starting youth programs. When Peter said "Friends," he meant Quakers.

"Hey," Peter says. "Thirsty?" He walks to the garden gate, holds up a bottle of cold water, and tosses it over the fence. "I thought the Neighborhood Association decided against turning this lot into a community garden."

"They did. Mr. Montgomery and I are doing it on our own. Lookit," I say and point to Mr. Montgomery's plot, 400 square feet of dark soil covered with manure. "They said rats would eat the vegetables. Is that true?"

"I have to get to the office," Peter says. "You be here tomorrow? I could help."

"Yeah, I'll be here." I assume he knows I like him, and presume his feelings are mutual, which is why he's offered to help. I get back to digging, and I dig fast, so that tomorrow we can plant.

I ponder how I'll invite him to drive with me out

to the county to buy tomato plants. We'll come back here to sow each one a foot deep, a foot apart. I'll hold up tall wooden stakes while he pounds them into the spongy earth with one fell stroke of a rock. Maybe if I cultivated relationships more carefully, as I cultivate this garden, I'd be happy now, and in a relationship with someone like Peter.

The next morning I arrive at the garden just as Mr. Montgomery is leaving. Tall and angular in a frayed khaki suit, he carries a hoe over his right shoulder. He has neatly tucked his dirty white shirt into his pants, which are held up with a rope through the belt loops. I imagine this is an old suit of his, something he wore to a downtown office in the seventies. "Been churning the manure deeper," he says.

I hold up an egg carton filled with seedlings already flopping in the sun.

"Why, it's too early, Son. Gonna get chilly again and might frost over."

Peter drives up. Mr. Montgomery tips his straw hat and nods; he holds the gate open wide for Peter then locks us in. Peter and I spread manure into the dark soil. I ignore Mr. Montgomery's warning, and meticulously plant the sprouts. "Lettuces like the cold," I explain to Peter. Conversation flows between us while we work.

"I want you to meet her…" Peter is saying. I am hearing for the first time about his wife and two daughters, parochial school, little girls' unique names. Has he never mentioned them before, or have I not heard him?

I can turn a dreary soup kitchen into a thriving community center, start an after-school program where there was none, and I can hear vegetables ripen, but when I'm besotted with a man I heed none of the truth, nor perceive any of the secrets. I'm too busy holding back an infatuated "I love you" in the first few weeks while I look ahead recklessly to a rosy future. It's like planting too early. I toss the rest of the drooping shoots into the ground and turn them under with the manure.

Peter gets busy in another neighborhood and I see less of him. My days take on a soothing monotony and rhythm: gardening in the morning, and hanging around the community center in the afternoon for kids' programs. In the evening, the soup kitchen runs smoothly without my supervision. By early May the cooks are serving Mr. Montgomery's greens at the nightly meal. A couple of folks who eat there ask if they can have garden plots, too. The president of the community association tells me how pleased she is with my work.

Still, I feel incomplete, abandoned, and lonely. I often go home after work just to watch "must-not-see" TV, eat too much popcorn for dinner, and go to bed early, bloated, sad, and confused about what I am sad about. One Wednesday I decide to drive across town to O'Donnell Square in south Baltimore to meet with the Frontrunners, a gay running club I belong to. Mike is the only one there. I've seen him at a few runs, but we've never run together. He's with the seven-minute-mile group, and has the thin ropey body of a long distance runner. He's wearing old style running shorts and stretched out socks; his legs are solidly muscular. Skinny arms stick out of a dingy tee-shirt from a 10K race in St. George, Utah.

A chilly wind sweeps up from the bay. At the appointed time to begin a five mile run along the harbor, no other club members have shown up. I admit shyly, "I run a ten-minute mile."

"That's fine," he says, and beams me a smile.

He trots alongside me, and sets a quick tempo with short strides. We talk about how we got started in Frontrunners, where we live, what we do. He works for the Internal Revenue Service. Every few minutes he asks, "How's this pace for you?"

The tempo remains regular and our breathing is even as we discover we were both English majors. He tells me how he ended up in a government job twenty-five years ago. I talk about the center. Conversation moves on to William Least Heat Moon, and Wallace Stegner. His favorite author is Dreiser, and mine, at the moment, is Nuala O'Faolain.

"What are you reading, now?" Mike asks.

"*The Farewell Symphony*, by Edmund White."

"Me, too. How's this pace for you?"

"You're reading *Farewell Symphony*? That's a coincidence, isn't it?"

"Not really. This pace okay?"

"Perfect," I say.

Mike brings up the Book Festival next weekend. "Let's go together," he says.

He picks me up in a clean white Subaru. I'm surprised to see Mardi Gras beads dangling from the rearview mirror. I mention it and remember a weekend of debauchery in the French Quarter while he talks about his favorite musicians and restaurants.

He knows more about books than I do, and shares facts in an unpretentious way. I want to relax and stop trying to impress him with my knowledge, my finesse, my amiability. How could I be forty-eight years old and never have been out with a man as simple, nice, and bright as he is? Not that this is a date. It isn't, is it?

A couple of weeks later, my friends call with extra theatre tickets; Mike and I join them. That night he wears dress pants and a checkered sport coat in pretty shades of gold. I wear jeans and a blue blazer, as usual. Later my friends say we look good together.

I tell them, "We're just friends. He's not my type." I made up my mind about that when he didn't respond to my brushing up against him while we shuffled with the crowd into theatre lobby, and when he never touched my elbow while it hung on the arm rest between us throughout the play.

"Why not your type?" my friend, Stacey, squeals.

He's not aggressive enough, not mean enough, dumb enough, or unavailable enough, I think sardonically. "He just isn't," I say. "It's instinct. Leave me alone."

That summer the tomatoes are abundant and tasty. Mr. Montgomery eats them like apples. We use them in the salads at the soup kitchen, and dish up large helpings of okra, peppers, and spaghetti squash, also from the garden. I share my herbs with Mr. Montgomery and the other two gardeners. I take the moonflower seeds that Mr. Montgomery gives me although I have no intention of sowing them. They'd take over.

"Look at them," Mr. Montgomery says early one morning pointing to the showy white blooms. They're my favorite. What're yours?"

"I don't know." Melancholy seeps into me as I realize I have no flower, no one, to call my favorite. "I think I like the miniature zinnias." Dwarfed, neat, and compacted.

"They're nice, too, I reckon," he says halfheartedly.

While I weed my plot I think about how I find moonflowers too wild, too messy. Is this how I feel about Mike? Afraid my feelings will take over? Get messy? I let these questions close up like moonflowers do in the early morning sun.

Mike and I run together on a Wednesday night in autumn. I am breathing hard. He's talking about the Cone Collection he saw at the Baltimore Museum of Art, with Olaf, another Frontrunner.

"Slow down. You're running too fast," I say. I wonder if it was a date.

Mike's now reporting, "The Frontrunner Halloween party is this Friday night. Shall I pick you up? Is this pace okay?"

I blurt out, "I can see the Marlborough from my living room. Where they lived, the Cone sisters," and pry, "Where's Olaf from, anyway; do you know?"

At the Halloween party I sit next to Mike on a soft leather couch. When I make room for others, I let the middle cushion dump me against Mike as if we were in a big old car making a wide turn. I feel his warmth. Is this a date? Would we kiss goodnight?

No. He drops me off, as usual. It's chilly, and the stars are hardly visible in the dark October sky. Mike waits to drive away, as he always does, until I get inside the house. I wave, but he doesn't see me.

We go to the movies once or twice and for a couple

of hikes before Mike leaves for Milwaukee to visit his family for Christmas and New Year's Eve. He calls me soon after he gets back to Baltimore. We go to hear Edmund White speak on Proust at the Smithsonian.

Edmund White is impish, plump, and pedantic. I am disappointed that he says nothing to help me understand my feelings for Mike. Didn't Proust know everything about longing? Stacey thinks I'm falling in love with Mike and that I'm afraid to tell him. Is she right?

Mike says White was insightful, and an excellent speaker. "What did you find pedantic about him?" he asks me.

Things slow down between us after that. "Tax season," Mike says. The days are dry and cold and windy; the rest of the winter drags on. But spring comes early and I'm ready to go to work in the garden as soon as Mr. Montgomery declares it's okay to turn over the soil.

I see Mike at Frontrunners on a Saturday morning in April. He looks different; his hair is longer, his face tan. I hadn't noticed before how handsome. I study the slant of his brow, the bow of his nose. He says, "What do you have cooking today?"

"I'm working in the garden."

"Want some help? I have tools."

"Yeah," I say. We smile. I think Stacey was right.

I like the familiar sound of the clacking beads as we drive to the garden together. Mr. Montgomery is already there. Mike and I unload two shovels, a rake, and a galvanized watering can. Mr. Montgomery meets us at the locked gate. He tips his hat, and introduces himself to Mike, "Pleasant Montgomery."

Mike introduces himself, and they shake hands. Later as we're all working near each other, Mike asks Mr. Montgomery how he got his name.

"I got it the minute my mama set eyes on me, Mr. Mike."

After he left, Mike says, "He's a real gentleman, isn't he?"

"And he has a gentleman's garden. Flowers and vegetables mixed. You got to be a gentleman to use some of your good land for flowers."

"Is ours a gentleman's garden?"

"Not until we plant flowers. We could collect seeds from Mr. Montgomery's garden."

"What are those?" he says.

"Moonflowers. They bloom at night. They open up in one minute, and close when the sun hits them in the morning."

"That's romantic," he says.

That's what I think. We gather handfuls of creamy white seeds from last season's dark dry pods and plant them along the fence at the back of the garden.

One hot evening in June, I walk to the Center on the shady side of the street. Through her curtained windows, I see a friend, Miss Mitchell, sitting in her wheelchair in the first floor apartment of an empty building. She's lived in this large red brick building for over thirty years. "I'm not about to move now, since I got my other leg cut off," she told me once. A geranium, already lanky, grows on the fire escape in the shade. I wave, but she can't see me; I don't knock, lest I scare her.

A man called Pork Chop limps up the street, dragging

a garbage can. When I say, "Hi," he nods. He sweeps the gutters every morning and evening, fills up his pail with Dixie cups and paper plates from the center, and with barrettes, bottle caps, and chicken boxes full of bones sucked clean.

Boys ride by on bikes too small for them, scouting for cops, and calling out "Five-oh" when they spot them. One of them calls out to me, "Whatchew looking for?"

"I'm on my way to the Res Hill Community Center; the 800 block." I point.

"You the police." He says *po*lice with the accent on "po."

"I'm not the police." I say it the other way. I feel scared; remember stories I've heard about people who "dis" these guys.

"I ain't asking, I'm telling. You the police."

"Leave the man alone," Pork Chop shouts. He turns around and begins to amble back toward us.

"Stay the fuck away, Five-oh," the boy says to me. He pops a wheelie and rides away laughing. "Yo," he calls out. "He ain't the police. Po'k Chop the police."

Later, when I see Mr. Montgomery at the garden, I tell him what happened. "You best be scared; those boys don't play. They don't think about the consequences of killing a white man up here."

For the next several days, I walk five blocks out of my way to avoid the corner of Whitelock and Lakeview Streets. I hold my head down so that I won't catch the eyes of boys on bikes. I have to admit I am fearful of them, just like everyone else in the neighborhood. All these months I've been scared of moonflowers, scared of asking a man I like, and who likes me, out on a date. Now I'm being challenged by something real, and wonder if I have the courage to stay in Reservoir Hill to do the work of the center.

Eventually, my anxiety begins to lessen. On a particularly summery evening I decide to call Mike at his office and ask as nonchalantly as I can, "How about dinner? We could call it a date."

"Okay," he says. I hear enthusiasm in his voice.

After dinner we drive over to the garden. Everything is up, green, fresh, full, lush. Ants navigate their way up and down the rose bushes; mint's in bloom and already going to seed among the bees. I stroke some rosemary and carry its heady smell on my fingers over to Mike's nose. I feel his breath. We pick a warm tomato.

"Want a taste?"

Mike drops the whole thing into his mouth at once.

Mr. Montgomery is picking beans. He's wearing seersucker suit pants and his straw hat. He takes it off when we get close. "Evening," he says. "I just finished watering, Mr. Rick. I noticed moonflowers coming up in your garden against the fence."

Mike and I say, "A gentleman's garden," at the same time, a little out of sync.

"That's real good," he says.

I ask them if they want to take a walk over to the community center with me. Folks are out on their porches, sitting on steps, standing on the sidewalk. "Good evening, gentlemen," small groups of them say to the three of us at once.

"Good evening," we answer.

The sun is still bright and high in a blue sky. Miss Mitchell's red geranium is vivid in the early evening light; she sits in her window like a queen, and waves to us. The boys are changing shifts at the drug market. The whole crew has moved around the corner to languish on the stoops while business is slow, until it gets dark.

Pork Chop is sweeping the gutter. "That man's been cleaning up the 800 block of Whitelock his whole life," Mr. Montgomery tells us. "How's everything, Mr. Wilson?" he inquires of the man I have known only as Pork Chop.

"Everything's good here, Mr. Montgomery. How's your garden?"

"Oh, the gardens are good this year. Mr. Rick here and Mr. Mike have got themselves a fine gentleman's garden. Why don't you come by?"

We poke our heads into the soup kitchen. It's lively and friendly in there. They're serving fried chicken, Mr. Montgomery's greens, and my tomatoes. Mr. Montgomery decides to stay for dinner. A paper cup of red, orange, and yellow zinnias has been placed in the center of each table.

Mike and I walk back up Whitelock. When bike riders pass us, Mike calls out, "Hi." They call "Hi" back at us. When I brush up against him, he brushes back up against me. I don't feel afraid anymore.

"I want to hold your hand, or put my arm around you," I tell him.

He hangs his arm around my shoulders. We walk by the garden without stopping in, and make our way to my house. Like moonflowers, we've bloomed at the end of our day and will remain open now throughout the night.

Rick Connor lives in Baltimore, Maryland. He is a member of The Writer's Center in Bethesda, Maryland, and of the Creative Alliance in Baltimore where he took his first "Write Here, Write Now" workshop in fall 2006. Rick's stories have appeared in City Paper, the Urbanite, *and* Divided City.

The Glider, Endings, The Wooden Box

M. Kathy Spath

My bad sense of direction led me to you. Having just heaved an old upholstered brown chair into its proper receptacle, I was intending to head home but, instead of using the road out of the dump, I tangled my way into its bowels.

I see you sitting there so proud and alone, with white paint rusting on your arms. You sit in front of a small white building, waiting for someone, perhaps? Are you for the taking or part of the scenery?

I remember having one like you. Years ago, I glided on our porch's smooth red tiles on Pelham Avenue in Baltimore City. I remember beige scrolls of metal attached to a wooden seat, and steel hardware that reinforced your base.

Glide. Nothing so peaceful as a body rhythmically gliding on a Saturday summer's afternoon. Back and forth. Tap. Tap. My feet touch the wooden porch. Around me lawns are being trimmed inside their postage stamp borders, and curbs are being jumped by bicycling boys with sheer delight. My neighbor waves. She's parading Derek and Darrell out their front door, just steps away. My husband and I call them "Darrell and his other brother Darrell." These characters came from some writer's imagination, used in an old sitcom. I look for any movement from across the street at 2834. Venetian blinds do double duty at this neighbor's home. "What does he have to hide?" I ask myself. The guy who lives there seems quite plain—ash brown hair, wire rimmed glasses, khaki pants, and white tennis shoes. Surely nothing to get one's blood in a stir, but who am I to judge?

Nothing like gliding on a glider on a Saturday afternoon. Back and forth. Tap. Tap. My feet touch down and rise on the backslide, much like swinging, only slower.

I realize my little son, Julian, has been over at the Parr's house playing on the swings for over an hour now. "I'd better check on him," I say aloud.

The Parrs are great neighbors and even greater friends. Their cozy home is filled with arts and crafts. Carl builds wooden children's chairs out of pine, carves wooden Rudolph's decorations for the holidays, and assembles little elephant toothbrush holders, complete with your child's name painted on it. My son has one.

I meander across the street to their house. As I knock on the door, I see Theresa Parr, lift her weight up from the blue colonial type sofa. She opens the locked screen door for me, then without a word trots to the back of the house, and heads outside.

"Julian...your mom's here," she yells to him. She pats Julian on the head as he enters the dining room and blurts out, "THAT RED HAIR...the kids are gonna call you 'carrot top.'"

Julian's too young to comprehend. He asks me, "Mom, will I have a carrot growin' outta my head?" with a puzzled frown on his face.

I chuckle. "No, sweetheart. Carrot top means you have red hair."

"But Mom, you always say I have *orange* hair, not RED hair."

"Yes, I do tell you that, Julian."

We all begin laughing. I wish I could catch each of these precious moments and roll them into a big ball. When I'd unwind it, all the memories could roll back to me.

"Is Ashley here?" I ask Theresa. Ashley is Theresa's precocious granddaughter, and the same age as Julian.

"She's in the yard with Dee." Dee is Theresa's youngest adult daughter.

"Would you mind watching Julian for another half an hour or so? I'll be back around two o'clock."

"No problem. These two get along real good as long as Ashley gets her way."

"See ya' later," I say as I slam the front screen door.

I walk back across the one-way street, and prance up to my front porch and the glider. Again we move back and forth. Back and forth. Tap. Tap.

And, now a truck rolls by the dump and interrupts my daydream. I look at you one more time, before I wave goodbye.

Endings

Let me tell you about my sister-in-law, Maxine. She's practically dead in my eyes.

During one of our one and a half hour long, long distance telephone conversations, she said to me, *If I visit someone's house and it's messy, I won't go back...I won't go back.*

Just like that. Period. The end. I felt my eyes bulge out of my head in disbelief.

As usual, I didn't have time for a response, as she began rambling on about one of her ex-students from Our Lady of the Queen of the Lakes. A rich parochial school in a rich neighborhood. I was still hooked on this messy house thing, which took me for a loop. It was as if she'd coiled a phone cord around me, and I was left hanging on for dear life. At first, I assumed she was talking about her eldest daughter, Suzanne. Suzanne and her family have five or six junk cars in their front yard, lined up haphazardly around their driveway. And Maxine seldom traveled fifteen minutes to their house, even though Suzanne doesn't have a working car to drive.

A few months later, it dawned on me that I wasn't a Martha Stewart kind of housekeeper per se. I'm, or should I say, my husband, son, and I are more like junk room junkies, our house is the kind of place where someone needs to clear the bed before sleep, or you'll end up with a book by Ann Tyler poking you in the back, or a box of Ritz crackers if you're hungry, and be careful walking through my son's room—there's no path—or...

Was Maxine also speaking to me in an indirect way? Is that why she and my brother don't come to visit when they travel to Baltimore? Because of the messy house syndrome?

After that, our relationship changed so much that she stopped calling me for our marathon phone conversations. So, I waited and waited, calling her occasionally, and then I got her back. I stopped phoning her! The minute I stopped calling her, our phone conversations ceased forever, or so it seems. The end.

Still, I ask myself, *How could I be so blind...so stupid... so messy?*

This cord-cutting happens after knowing this

woman forty six years of my life. That's a long time to know someone and then have them turn their back on you. For so many years we were so close. She was like a sister to me.

I was only eight years old with a brown pixie haircut, wearing a striped shirt and plaid shorts when we met. She resembled Jackie Kennedy—dark brunette hair falling to her shoulders, her body slim, and a smile for the world. I'd run up to my dad's car, as Pete, my oldest brother, and Maxine, his soon-to-be bride, sat in the car, just ready to take off to her house.

*Wait...*I'd say. *Please, please take me with you.*

Pete would grin at Maxine, while she stepped from the car to lift the front seat so I could sit in the back.

I'd yell, *Mom, I'm going with them.*

Okay, she'd say. *Mind your manners.*

And we'd take off to Hamilton, about a ten minute ride from our house to theirs. Once there, I'd play with Maxine's sister, Janet, who was three years my senior. One of our favorite pastimes was to sing old Beatles songs, like: *I Want to Hold Your Hand,* or later, *Yellow Submarine.*

So, this went on, these excursions. Maxine was as much a part of our family as I was, maybe even too much so. My mother seemed to drool over Maxine's every move, every word. Maxine's mouth moved faster in five minutes than mine moved in one whole day. She'd tell us about their friend, Brent, who lived on the north Charles Street side of town, about Pat McCourt who was going to be her bridesmaid and wear a chiffon powder blue gown in the wedding. Of course, I wasn't going to be in it. My mother thought Maxine knew everything because she had that 'gift of gab,' unlike her own daughter, me.

During the summer we went on family vacations together to Ocean City, after the marriage and children, of course. We went swimming in the vast Atlantic Ocean. One particular summer, after fifteen years had passed, we found ourselves in the ocean again, with my dad close by. The waves pounded the shore as they announced their arrival inland. We walked out as far as we could to bob the waves before they knocked us down in their rage and fury. Eventually, the sand became mushy, and the undertow was becoming a strong force at our feet, pulling us out of our way. All of the sudden Maxine grabbed onto my arm, nearly pulling me down with her. Her brown eyes looked at mine with a trepidation that cannot be described. I took her hand.

Lets go back, I said. *Just hold my hand tight, and we'll be okay.*

As we returned to shore with my dad, all of us seemed to be huffing and puffing our way back to the blankets.

I asked Maxine, *Are you okay? What happened to you? I know it was a bit rough out there, but...*

I get panic attacks.

Panic attacks?

Yes. I get afraid when I don't have control over a situation. I didn't have control out there.

Are you seeing a doctor for this?

I just saw my family doctor recently. He's prescribing some anti-anxiety medicine for me.

Oh, well I hope it turns out okay for you.

Each year or two, I visited their home, which was

neat as a pin and located in Medford, New Jersey, about two and a half hour drive from Baltimore. I enjoyed seeing my nieces—the three S's...Suzanne, (my favorite), Shelley, and Stephanie, as well as their children. The family kept growing.

Maybe that's part of what happened to our relationship. The family kept growing so large that there was no room or time for a sister-in-law. My brother and I have now begun an online e-mail relationship. This consists of humorous one liners, interesting pictures, or one-on-one political battle.

Whatever the real cause of the end of Maxine's and my relationship, it makes me sad. I have simply given up on the sister-in-law part of this. And, maybe I'm as guilty as she, closing the door on a once *happy* relationship. Endings are never easy to swallow, especially if they're salty.

The Wooden Box

A stack of six vintage cigar boxes sit on the antique store's wooden plank floor ready for the taking at fifteen dollars a piece. *Not good enough for him.*

I approach the clerk in Foley's Antique Store and inform him of the kind of box I'm searching for. Details are sketchy because I'm not certain myself. We look in the front of the shop full of old oak and mahogany furniture, then meander towards the back where the clerk spots a brown wooden box. After he blows the dust off, he hands it to me. I hold it as if it's a treasure box filled with life-long secrets. Its heavy, gnarled wood pleases me—blonde arcs of color blend with the brown wood; I'm delighted by its presence.

As I hold the box to my nose, the scent of musty perfume springs into my nostrils like the blossom of old age. My fingers stroke its grittiness. Like the salty flesh of some old sea captain in need of a bath.

This brown box beckons me. It longs to tell me a story. Before its hermitage in Foley's Antiques, it has fallen into the hands of others. Names and addresses are still a part of the box's design. On its surface, is written:

FROM: CAPTAIN ANTHONY S. CORINA,
NEW YORK

TO: MRS. JAMES W. SLICK,
BALTIMORE, MD

The black capital letters are neatly painted on the upright side of the box, an indelible mark of history. With Baltimore being my hometown, the mystery of the private lives of these two people intrigues me. Not that I'm driven to the point of digging up wads of historical information, I'm simply curious. I notice there is no zone or zip code information, so, this was a time prior to the use of such zones.

I slide the top of the box towards the right, opening a whiff of its age. It smells a bit like this antique store, musty and old. On the front side of the box, I discover a tattered yellowish piece of paper taped there. It reads: *Property of the United States Government.* Further down, a name appears in sketchy penmanship, *Jack Cockran* with an indecipherable rank underneath.

I admire how the box is precisely constructed,

especially the wooden dovetailed corners. Just the fact that this box is *still* functional says something about the carpenter's skill. Surpisingly, the postal service hasn't destroyed it by now! I can't help but wonder how many others have held this box. Did they mail something practical inside it, like dish cloths, or something sexy and extravagant, like silk stockings? Did they mail their parcel to a husband, a wife, a friend, a lover, or a brother? What treasures were placed inside this box after its receipt—jewelry, love letters, paper money, or silver coins?

This box is a gift for my girlfriend's brother, Tony. He and his sister, Valerie, have been close friends for thirty years. The last time I visited them in Colorado, Tony's crazy ways helped boost Valerie's and my spirits, for she's been sick with appendix cancer, a rare form of the disease. I traveled from the other side of the country to be with her. Tony travels two and one-half hours to reach Colorado Springs where her husband and stepson live.

During my visit, when Valerie's body grew tired or she was busy with work, Tony took time to drive me through the Rocky Mountains. What mountains! They were breathtaking dark forms of rock looming over the towns and cities. Tony sped his big blue truck through the curves. I covered my face with my hands, then peeked through the cracks. He let out a pretend scream. We sang old rock and roll tunes like: *A Crazy Little Thing Called Love* by the late Elvis Presley and then laughed at the sound of our voices deep in the tenor of offbeat living.

Later that evening, Tony attempted to persuade me

to gamble with him on the dogs. I told him, *I can't do that.* The greyhounds aren't running in Loveland, but in Denver, so a simulcast is broadcasted inside the track building. Gambling on greyhounds running the oval track wasn't easy for me. I saved two precious greyhounds from death. I wish I could save Valerie.

After two surgeries, three months of failed chemotherapy (the cancer grew instead of shrunk), and boundless disappointment, she has now decided to see an alternative doctor in Colorado. We don't know for sure how long she has to live. It could be six months to a year, or less. The doctor's aren't talking. Only her Jesus truly knows, and he's not talking either. There's one positive spin to all this—Valerie is a fighter.

The thought of her impending death sends my emotions reeling like a cyclone. Though our thirty-year relationship has waxed and waned through failed marriages, hippiedom, disco duck, children, and many miles in between, it has survived.

She is the closest living relative to Tony. The rest are in Florida. I feel sorry for him, and wish he'd find someone to fill that void of love in his life. If I wasn't married...

Getting back to the names inscribed on the box, the ones in black paint are curiously similar to those in my own life. The box is addressed to Baltimore, where I live. The woman's name is Mrs. James W. Slick. James is my husband's first name. It's being sent by Captain Anthony Corina, the first name of the person I'm sending the box to is Anthony, or Tony.

Does coincidence play a part in these names, and in me buying this wooden box for Tony? I can't help but believe there is an unknown force or destiny that has a secret to reveal to me. But, what is it?

Although I don't now know the answer, maybe I will someday.

In the meantime, the following inscription I wrote is to be included inside the box for Tony:

> This is a gift for you. Let it carry the sunshine and struggles in your life. Let it lift your soul, when your soul needs lifting. Let it smile upon you when your voice needs laughter. Let it give rise to vivid imagination when you are at a loss for song. And, last, let it forever be a piece of you and me.
> Love,
> Kathy

M. Kathy Spath, born and raised in Baltimore, has been writing since the 1980s. She is presently working as a substitute teacher in Baltimore County schools. Kathy likes to write poetry and creative nonfiction, bowl, work with the elderly, and travel.

Goodbye, Francis

Tamara Keurejian

I have a love/hate relationship with the month of December. A certain poet may have pegged April as the cruelest month, but for me it will always be December because along with the frenetic, festive pace of the holiday season, there is one event from my past that haunts me, that I've never come to terms with—the day I killed a man.

It happened on a frigid night, eight years ago, a night so bitter cold the hair inside your nose turned brittle and it hurt to breathe. A night old men should have been warm and secure inside the safe confines of their homes. But Francis McLean, 88 years old and on foot, decided that was the night to cross a five lane highway. And he almost made it until I appeared, like a modern-day angel of death in my Jeep Cherokee. I'd actually been thinking of trading in the Jeep for something more fuel efficient, when Mr. McLean inadvertently helped make my decision. Believe me, if I could have done it any other way I would have. But sometimes the fates step in and there's nothing you can do but be witness to the surreal horror of metal and chrome slamming into flesh and blood at forty miles per hour.

Jesus Christ, I never saw him! It was like he fell from the fucking sky…I was driving and talking to Jordan, saying no honey, mommy can't turn around right now. And then he's on the hood of my car…and the heart-stopping thud of the impact…and he looked right at me and he had blue eyes…and then he was gone…

The shock and disbelief in his eyes remains imbedded in my mind to this day. My own unbelieving brown eyes stared right back at him, not comprehending I was the last image he'd ever see again.

I like to think Francis ventured out that evening believing he'd return home, safe and sound. It was his daughter's birthday the next day and he'd simply wanted to buy her a present, but no one was home to drive him to the store. His driver's license had been taken away by his family. They were afraid he'd get into an accident.

…and I pull over and run from the Jeep and he's curled up on the ground and no sound…no blood. An older woman in a green coat runs up to me. A frantic man screams into a cell phone. Jordan stay in the car, stay in the car. *Is that me yelling?* Go back to your daughter, *someone tells me.*

And then, somehow, I'm back in the Jeep, waiting for the police to arrive.

Until that evening, I'd never been inside a police cruiser or a precinct station. I'd only been pulled over once in my life for driving with a burned out brake light. Nary a speeding violation nor DUI blemished my driving record. So how in the hell did a day that started out with a matinee of *A Bug's Life* end up like this?

"Mr. Faulstich, your wife and daughter are fine, but there's been an accident…"

The only event my husband, Bruce, had anticipated that evening was a night out with the guys, his weekly ritual of pounding some pool balls and quaffing a few beers. The phone call from the county officer squashed those plans.

…And now Bruce is in the back seat of the police car with me and Jordan…How did he get here, how long has he been here…And now we're at the station and they take me to a room…but where's Jordan, who has her…

A plethora of jumbled thoughts ricocheted through my mind—I'm going to be arrested and charged, thrown in a holding cell till I can post bail. Bruce will need to get a lawyer, and Jordan will be taken from me. Finally, after what seemed like an hour, six hours, five minutes—who knows—an officer materialized. He wore plain clothes and had a bad comb-over; his face a neutral mask.

"Where is the man, where did they take him?" I manage to ask. My words were gritty sand, scratching up through my throat. "How is…is he…?" I couldn't articulate or finish the question.

"He's at the hospital," said the officer. "We don't know how he is yet, but we were able to notify his family. They should be there by now."

I looked to Bruce for something reassuring to hold onto, but he offered nothing tangible. A wife that ran down an old man was new territory for him. Stolid to begin with, in that moment he seemed more or less an accessory, like my purse sitting on the table next to me.

A blood alcohol test was requested and I submitted obligingly because the only drink I'd consumed was a super-sized diet coke. My sobriety was proven, ending any initial speculation that the tragedy happened under drunken circumstances. A second officer, younger and beefier, armed with pen and paper, jotted down what cryptic details I could provide. The most glaring question simply couldn't be answered: Why hadn't I seen him?

...No, I didn't turn around to talk to Jordan, wasn't playing with the radio or searching for something in my purse...My eyes, yes, they were focused straight ahead on the roadway...Both hands gripped to the wheel in the two and ten position...Never had a chance to hit the brakes...

Before the agonizing volley of questions and answers finally ceased, before Officer Bad Hair drove me, and my family, back to Bruce's car, Officer Beefy delivered the words I'd been dreading.

"He didn't make it. I'm sorry."

Mr. McLean was too old and fragile to sustain the massive internal injuries inflicted by a two thousand pound machine.

I heard a muffled cry from somewhere in the room and realized it emanated from me.

In the long days that followed, I hunkered down on the daybed in the third floor loft. A woman on a self-imposed exile. From under the tangle of musty sheets and blankets, I heard the life I once knew continue downstairs—Bruce in the kitchen making dinner, making a mess. Jordan in her room, playing with the new Christmas presents Santa had recently delivered. Sometimes she climbed the ladder to the loft and snuggled in tight beside me on the daybed. I felt her little arm around my waist, her head warm against my back. And I had to ask:

"Honey, do you remember anything from the other night?"

"I remember they gave me cookies and we watched TV."

Did she feel my palpable sigh of relief? There would be no more questions from me. If and when a flood of memories came to Jordan one day, I would answer them as best I could. But for now, let her enjoy the blissful ignorance of a five year old.

The phone rang occasionally and from Bruce's muffled responses it was evident I couldn't stay upstairs forever.

"No, I'm sorry. She can't come to phone right now." I heard him deflect yet another concerned friend or co-worker. "She'll call you when she's ready. Hey, before I forget, we're canceling the New Year's Eve party."

That's right I thought, eavesdropping from my safe nest-bed, an entire new year to anticipate. The enormity of it only cocooned me deeper into the blankets.

In between rounds of fitful sleep, I considered the parting advice of the younger officer from the night of the accident.

"You're going to be hit with all kinds of emotions," he'd warned. "You may want to talk to someone. Don't watch the news tonight, either."

Simmering just beneath my own grief was the fact that another family had also been devastated by this tragedy. Strangers who lived somewhere across town and had actual physical evidence to lay to rest and grieve—Francis Xavier McLean, beloved father and grandfather. A man I'm sure they'd envisioned dying peacefully in his bed after a long and happy life, all of them gathered around him. Not in the cold, stark emergency room of a large suburban hospital, his insides battered and bleeding. Initially, I'd wanted to contact them, let them know how sorry I was for being the one behind the wheel. This was discouraged, however, by my police buddies who checked in on me daily, as their investigation proceeded.

"The family doesn't blame you," they said. "They know it was an accident."

"But it seems so wrong to not say *anything*," I insisted.

"Okay, until we know for sure what happened just keep it simple. *Do not* apologize for anything."

My relief and shame intermingled when I realized there was no immediate need to meet the family face to face. Eventually I did send a letter (and never heard back from them), but at the time there was just one person I had to confront: me.

The vast expanse of the Sheppard Pratt medical complex could easily pass for a college campus, not a facility that catered to the needs of the emotionally damaged, drug or alcohol addicted, and mentally ill. From the moment I rolled my rental car (the Jeep was gone for good, thank God) through the arch of the hospital's stone gatehouse, I was relieved to see a charming backdrop of winter-weary trees surrounding modern buildings. I drove slowly, trying not to miss the Center for Post Traumatic Stress Disorders. I wasn't sure if that was what ailed me, but they'd had a last minute cancellation and it wasn't fair to lay the entire length of my emotional wreckage on my equally shell-shocked husband.

Bruce's apparent motto during times of crisis was "out of sight, out of mind." And with me conveniently tucked away up in the loft, exorcising my ghosts, he could proceed down below, hoping this whole mess would resolve itself, somehow. But still he tried, offering me comfort food and stilted words.

"At least he was old and not a kid," he said, or "He shouldn't have been out there walking around, anyway."

It was the best he could do at the time. What was offered in a medical context wasn't much better.

"So tell me, why are you here?" My "therapist" was a petite, crisp woman attired in various shades of black and gray. I wondered if she dressed this way everyday to match the monochromatic theme of her sparse office. She didn't possess a warm, fuzzy demeanor, which seemed odd for someone dealing with patients in distress. I'd been hoping for a warm grandma-type to pull me to her huge bosom and tell me it would all be okay.

"I was driving last week and hit and killed an elderly man," I said. There, it was out in the open at last.

"Were you arrested?" she asked. "Were you charged with anything?"

"No. The police say it's probably pedestrian error but they're still investigating." I was sweating even though it was early January.

"Mrs. Faulstich, what do you hope to get from these sessions?" Her dark-eyed stare was unnerving.

"I'd like to be able to figure out why I didn't see him," I admitted. "I'd like to get a good night's sleep again." I could feel my chest constricting. Was I giving her the answers she wanted?

"You do understand if you reveal any incriminating evidence I'll have to inform the police."

I was stunned. This was a woman who was supposed to *help* me? The urge to bolt through the door was overwhelming, though I fought it and stayed for the remaining hour. It was, however, my first and last appointment.

The passing of eight Decembers can easily disguise a lot of emotional scar tissue. My life is now segmented into halves: before I killed Francis, and after. I should have said my goodbyes and made peace with this a long, long time ago. I've carried him around all these years like a phantom limb, unseen but felt. It's time to cut him loose and set him (and me) free. And I want to scream "would someone please show me how!"

I'm not ready yet, but one day I'll wrangle up the nerve and venture out to the Dulaney Valley Memorial Gardens, walk into the caretaker's office and politely inquire as to the whereabouts of the late Francis McLean. I envision myself with directions in hand, returning to the car and driving with some trepidation to the gravesite, wondering why it took me so long to get here. I'll park (take a moment to organize my thoughts) and (with a good cleansing breath or two) manage to make my hands and fingers work in unison to open the car door. And then Francis, I'll ease myself down on the cold grass over your final resting place and the two of us will have a long, much over-do, one-sided conversation. But if we could partake in clever dialogue I imagine it would center on what a pisser fate can be.

"Francis, I'm so sorry about all this, but I have to ask. Why were you trying to cross five lanes of traffic without a light or crosswalk?"

"Bad move on my part, I admit. Don't blame yourself dear, it wasn't your fault."

"Your granddaughter was going to take you shopping the next day for your daughter's birthday, but you just couldn't wait, could you?"

"Next time, I'll listen."

"Do you have any idea what you put me through? What I've had to deal with these past eight years?"

"Oh, I get it…it's all about *you*?"

Yes, I'll acknowledge the anger didn't make any sense, But that was how I felt in the days that followed the accident (it *was* pedestrian error. Took them a month, but the police confirmed it). One of those mid-level stages of the grief process, I guess. At your graveside, Francis, I'll tell you time has helped dissipate the anger, put it in its proper place, laid it to rest.

We were two people simply maneuvering through life's daily events, I'll reflect, when harsh reality knocked both of us (you literally) on our asses. So Francis, I know you're not going anywhere, and one December, my cruelest month, I will find you. Maybe bring a couple bottles of good Irish ale (I'm going on the assumption that being the good Irish Catholic boy you once were, you'd have enjoyed belting a couple of cold ones), and I can attempt to bring this saga to its long-awaited conclusion.

Perhaps on the day I visit it'll be overcast and like a sign from the great beyond the clouds will part, the sun will emerge, and a warm deluge of comprehension will surge through me. The understanding that sometimes there are events we have no control over. We have no say so, we have no rights, no warning. They will happen whether we like it or not. Whether it's fair, or not.

Tamara Keurejian writes (or tries too, anyway) from a small corner in her Fells Point home. This was her first encounter with a writing workshop. She's not quitting her day job just yet.

Write Here, Write Now

10 Minute Plays

Revolvers

Leo Horrigan

SCENE: Stage is dark. Recorded tape plays of workers chanting "No justice … no peace" Tape plays for four or five seconds before …Lights come up. (Tape fades out.) JORGE holds the microphone while ANITA primps him, getting him ready to be on camera. JORGE looks fondly at the microphone as he turns it in his hands. CHET introduces story from the "studio."

ANITA

Remember, this is television … snappy answers … no speechifying … Don't get all … philosophical on me.
(JORGE nods.)
We're down to five seconds. You OK?
(JORGE nods. ANITA takes microphone.)
Just follow my lead.

CHET

Shoppers are enduring great hardship this holiday weekend, ever since a gang of workers took over a local Sprawl Mart. Now, a WDUL Eye Team reporter is IN the locked-down store on Commercial Way. Anita, what's all the fuss?

ANITA

That's still unclear, Chet. These workers have a laundry list of complaints, but no clear message. Yet, they are determined to ride out this crisis, quote, "for as long as it takes."

CHET

As long as it takes to do what, Anita?

ANITA

Let me ask Jorge Candu. What do you and your accomplices hope to achieve while inconveniencing so many Sprawl-Mart shoppers?

JORGE

We want to put the bosses on notice that we won't tolerate any more unpaid overtime, sexual harassment of women employees, or firings without cause.

ANITA

Soooooo, what's your point?

JORGE

We won't work for poverty wages anymore, and we are reclaiming our dignity. No compromise in defense of workers' rights!

ANITA

Well, our viewers know how much this strike has disrupted holiday plans for so many area families. Chet, I understand you have more on that situation.

CHET

Anita, one local man waited *two and a half hours* in the parking lot, hoping to buy charcoal briquets for a family cookout. Finally, he drove *eleven miles* to the nearest Shoppers' Paradise so his family would not have to do without.

ANITA

That story tore me up.

JORGE

We don't want to inconvenience anyone. We just want some respect for—

ANITA

Well, there you have it, Chet. It seems that a seething, unfocused anger has taken over this workforce, fueled by a demagogic and incendiary leader. This is likely to explode into a violent bloodbath—possibly by 11 p.m.

JORGE

Nobody's going to get violent. This is a peaceful protest.

ANITA

Ooooooh, it won't play like that.

CHET

Stay safe down there, Anita. Just remember, we've got your back.

ANITA

I'll try, Chet. But the situation seems to grow more tense by the instant. Workers are chanting "No justice, no peace." We all know what the opposite of peace is.

JORGE

This is just an express—

ANITA

Makeshift weapons abound in any Sprawl-Mart store. The hardware section alone is a paramilitary's dream. Throw in Home & Garden and you've got real trouble. I can picture angry workers toting pitch forks, trowels, weed whackers, flatware...

CHET

I don't want to picture it, Anita.

JORGE

But I work in women's apparel.

ANITA

Plenty of strangulation devices there.

CHET

Ouch! Death by thong doesn't sound pretty. All the more reason for the Eye Team to keep an eye on this story, Anita. Thanks for that report.

ANITA

All right, we're off air.

JORGE

Pleeeeease let me give my side of this!

ANITA

I think I've done a pretty good job of representing your views.

JORGE
(Reaches for microphone.)
Let me explain it all and you can edit out what you don't like.

ANITA

I'll do the explaining. You just answer my questions.

JORGE

I just want one shot at giving my side of things.
(Grabs for microphone again.)

ANITA

Don't you touch me, you animal! Somebody call for backup!

JORGE

I just wanna borrow it. Relax!
(Struggle over microphone ensues. Stage goes black. JORGE ties ANITA to a chair with a rope of nylons and gags her with women's underwear.)

> *JORGE dons her jacket.*
> *Lights up.)*

CHET

For the latest in the Sprawl-Mart controversy, we bring you back to Anita Tenchin, inside the store. What's happening over there, Anita?

JORGE

Ummmm, Anita's a little ... tied up right now. But I can give you an update.

CHET

Take your best shot, young man.

JORGE

Well, aaah, things have heated up here, Chet, just as WDUL News predicted earlier this evening. We have the woman in custody, and we expect to break the owners' resolve any day now.

> *(ANITA gestures wildly,*
> *spits out gag.)*

ANITA

Free Anita! No negotiation with terrorists!

JORGE

I'm not a terrorist. I'm a stock boy.

ANITA

That's what they all say. Why don't you go back where

you came from?

JORGE

To Glen Burnie? You can't make me.

CHET

Since you've got that microphone in your hand, Jorge, why don't you tell us a little about yourself.

ANITA

Don't coddle him, Chet—he's a dangerous man!

JORGE

Well, you see, my dad got me every other job I ever had —and fired me from my last one, at his company. So, I told him "I quit" and struck out on my own. I hope you're watching, Dad. Hi, Mom.

ANITA

Puh-leeze!

JORGE

Now I understand what you were always telling me, Dad—how you can't appreciate anything you get the easy way. That's why I'm willing to fight now, to improve the workers' plight. And I've never felt so alive in all my life!

(ANITA mocks
JORGE's speech.)

CHET

Once again, WDUL has brought you a newsmaker up close and personal, behind the headlines, past the cliches, beyond the soundbites—

ANITA

And over the hill to grandma's house. Have you noticed that I'm tied up here! Could ya throw me a bone?

CHET

On the next installment of …"The Media Held Hostage," WDUL will bring you the wrenching tale of an intrepid reporter who braved hostile workers and the threat of violence to bring us the real story behind the Sprawl-Mart lockout.

ANITA
(To herself.)

Much better.

CHET

Until then, stay tuned to WDUL for up-to-the-minute updates on the hostage crisis.

> *(PAPER GIRL enters, walks around stage holding up newspaper. Meanwhile, JORGE removes nylon "rope" around ANITA.)*

PAPER GIRL

Workers give Ten-chin a re-education!   *(two times)*

ANITA

(Speaks with eyes rolling back in her head.)

Welcome to Sprawl-Mart. Enjoy your shopping experience. Welcome to Sprawl-Mart. Enjoy… your shopping experience…Enjoy your shopping experience…

(JORGE begins to speak over her.)

JORGE

You see how they try to hypnotize us? The shoppers and the workers! Now, check out these statistics.

(JORGE holds up pamphlet titled "The Workers' Plight.")

ANITA

Six bucks an hour? I spend that much on nylons per hour.

(ANITA and JORGE freeze. PAPER GIRL enters.)

PAPER GIRL

TV hottie goes radical chic with Latino boy toy! *(two times)*

(ANITA holds up pamphlet.)

ANITA

I was up all night reading this. Suddenly I understand
what the struggle .... la lucha .... is all about.

JORGE

Now you've got to make it real.

ANITA

How do you mean?

JORGE

Look at what you're wearin', angel. Exploitation is
wrapped up in those threads. Your wretched global
sisters are crying out to you from every unseemly
seam.

> *(JORGE checks label on
> back of dress.)*

A hundred percent linen—and you got it on the cheap?
Get outta town, princess.

> *(ANITA sheds dress.)*

And what's this? Revolutionaries don't wear Victoria's
Secret. That's blood money, honey.

> *(JORGE pushes ANITA
> back into chair, removes
> her shoes.)*

Might as well lose the shoes, hermana. They smell like

a sweatshop I once knew.

(Stage goes black.)

ANITA

So la lucha is about getting naked?

JORGE

If I can't strip, it's not my revolution.
> *(Lights up. PAPER
> GIRL enters, walks
> around stage.
> Meanwhile, JORGE sits
> in chair and ANITA
> straddles him.)*

PAPER GIRL

Extra! Extra! 'DUL doll sheds it all for modern-day Che. *(two times)*

CHET

We are into Day 16 of "The Media Held Hostage" and well-wishes keep pouring in for Anita Tenchin. Let's return to the scene of the ongoing crime in the 52-thousand, 400 block of Commercial Way. WDUL brings you exclusive coverage of the Sprawl-Mart Liberation Army—out of the mouths of kidnappers and into your living rooms! *(Beat.)* One of our reporters is on top of the situation. Jorge, are you there?

JORGE
> *(Peeking around*

ANITA's hip.)

We're *both* here, Chet. And, yes, there's breaking news —the former reporter formerly known as Anita is formally free!

CHET

Long live Anita! Folks, WDUL has done it again. We've brought you the news as it happens, where it happens, when you need it, while you're watching, without—

ANITA

Enough!
(Pause.)
And it's not Anita, you windbag! I have shed that bourgeois label. Henceforth, I shall be known as Vencerema, Defender of the People.

CHET

At any rate, the world has been worried sick about you. We all want to know, Ani—, Venc—, miss, are those disgruntled workers treating you OK down there?

ANITA

Are you kidding? I've never felt so alive in all my life.
(Grabs JORGE and
kisses him on the lips.)
You tell your fascist pig bosses that the revolution is being televised!

CHET

They're your fascist pi—They're your bosses, too, Anita.

Remember that. Now, there have been rumors that you may have been brainwashed into supporting this strike.

                    ANITA
                              (Speaking like she is
                              hypnotized.)
Allegations that I have been brainwashed are ridiculous and beyond belief. And, if I WERE brainwashed, I must have had a dirty mind.
                              (Elbows JORGE. They
                              laugh.)

                    CHET
What would you like to tell your army of WDUL well-wishers who have stood by you throughout this ordeal?

ANITA
I'd like to speak directly to the people now—and tell them that I would never choose to live the rest of my life …
                              (CHET makes sounds of
                              static.)
… surrounded by corporate swine who exploit the reserve army of surplus labor for their own self—

                    CHET
We're having trouble hearing you. We'll have to break away for the five-day forecast.
                              (Steps out from behind
                              news desk, wearing

      boxers that say "Property
      of WDUL.")
What the heck's gotten into you, Anita? You know you
can't do long-winded speeches on TV.

      (Goes back to his desk.
      Sits down.)
This isn't theater, for cripe sakes. Do you wanna blow
your chance for a network job?

ANITA

Don't you see that I'm not your brown-nosin' side-
squeeze anymore? *(Beat.)* I'm Vencerema! Jorge has
helped me see the light. Right now, I'd like to send my
love out…

CHET

Save it …

ANITA

…to all of the workers toiling in the retail concentration
camps across this nation.

CHET

Come on now …

ANITA

…We're coming to rescue you from this corporate
dictatorship!

CHET

You're off the air, Anita. Save your energy.

JORGE

This reminds me, Vencerema, that some of us are concerned that your rhetoric is getting...overheated. We'd like to soften it a little.

ANITA

(Pacing.)

Edit my speeches, huh? Now you're afraid to ruffle a few feathers?

JORGE

Sometimes less is more.

ANITA

(Still pacing.)

Goddamn moderates are taking over. You won't catch me watering down the revolution for the sake of a little popularity.

CHET

Seems to me, Jorge's talkin' sense, Anita. Maybe there's hope for ending this stalemate.

ANITA

Butt out, Hairdo Boy! This is revolutionary business. And don't call me Anita!

CHET

I'm not sure what I ever saw in you—Anita! This Jorge guy broke a bigger story than you ever did. Maybe he's network material.

ANITA

Hello? I am the story he broke! And the network's gonna hire a kidnapper?

JORGE

Don't call me that. I'm a *former* kidnapper. What were you saying, Chet?

CHET

Well, Rodriguez is leaving nightcast for morning roundup. Network wants to fill his shoes with someone like you, if you know what I mean. I could talk you up, amigo.

JORGE

Would everybody please stop calling me amigo? But, yeah, I guess you could put in a word for me, Mr. Humpley.

(Pause. Turns to
ANITA.)

This could be my chance to really expose the workers' plight.

ANITA

Not on your life, Jorge. It won't play like that.

JORGE

(Staring off into space.)

I can finally prove myself worthy.

ANITA

I don't know what I ever saw in a sellout like you.

> *(PAPER GIRL
> enters, walks around
> stage. ANITA dons
> revolutionary beret,
> picks up megaphone.
> JORGE combs hair,
> dons sportcoat.)*

PAPER GIRL

Radical Hunk Goes Mainstream!   *(two times)*

CHET

As the Sprawl-Mart standoff grinds into its twenty-forth day, we bring you the latest from our newest WDUL reporter, George Kant. Welcome to the team, George. What have you got for us?

JORGE

The latest talks between management and workers have generated more heat than light, Chet. It seems that the most extreme element among the workers is now holding sway.

ANITA

> *Speaks through
> megaphone.)*

Don't believe the hype, people! The S-L-A is on its way!

JORGE
(*Pushes megaphone away.*)

This game of one-upmanship could last for weeks, even months, putting a crimp in two, maybe three, more holidays.

ANITA
(*Speaks through megaphone.*)

Soon, these workers will be free, and then we march on Shoppers' Paradise!

JORGE
(*Pushes megaphone away.*)

Speaking of Shoppers' Paradise, consumers should get there quick—and stock up on charcoal briquets... while there is still time.

CHET

There's some news you can use, folks. Just what you've come to expect from WDUL, your number one choice for local news for seven years running. We get it first, we get it right, we give it to you down the middle, hard and fast—

ANITA

Death to the fascist insect that preys upon the life of the people!

(*Stage goes black.*)

Leo Horrigan has worked as a reporter and copy editor in the newspaper industry, has helped forment urban agriculture projects in Baltimore, including a prison garden, and has written on topics in agriculture, public health, community food security, and environmental sustainability. His ten-minute play Slow Food *received a public reading in Boca Raton, Florida, in 2005. He lives in Baltimore with his wife, Margery McIver, and their nine-year-old dramatic and sporting son Eamon.*

Mouse Song

Ryan Whinnem

Setting: The kitchen of a home infested with mice.

Characters:

CAROLINE:	Alyson's friend. Late 20s, 30s. Nosy. Concerned
ALYSON:	Has problems. Late 20s, 30s. Can hear mice speaking to her.
SAMPULAMBIN:	Mouse. Looks like Alyson's ex-boyfriend. 20s, 30s. Self assured and a good singer.
JAMPERDAN:	Mouse. Only heard. Any age. Good backup singer. Likes Ham.
WAINSDUST:	Mouse. Only heard. Any age. Good backup singer. Likes cheerios.

The stage is a single table, a small kitchen table. There are two chairs. Some dirty dishes are piled upon the table, along with take out containers of various sorts and lengths of stay. In the middle of the table is a container of pills. A kitchen trash can stands in the corner. Alyson sits at the table, in her bathrobe, looking out at the audience. The phone rings. Alyson ignores it. Offstage, there is a knock. Alyson does not respond. A louder knock follows, and then a loud banging. Alyson looks up, exits offstage.

ALYSON (o.s.)

Caroline?

> *(Caroline enters,*
> *followed by Alyson)*

CAROLINE

You're not even dressed.

ALYSON

For what?

CAROLINE

For the Museum. I emailed you three days ago.

ALYSON

You did? Did I respond?

CAROLINE

Oh my God! Alyson! Look at this place.

ALYSON

Oh. I—

> *(Carolyn starts picking up the take out containers, walking them to the garbage can.)*

JAMPERDAN

She is disrupting the food supply!

WAINSDUST

Why does she disrupt the food supply?!

SAMPULAMBIN (SAM)

We must stop her.

ALYSON

Stop that!

SAM

Alyson protects us.

CAROLINE

Don't be silly. I'm helping you clean up.

ALYSON

Jesus, Caroline. Did I even fucking say, "come in"?

> *(Alyson starts taking the containers from*

*Caroline and setting
them back on the table.)*

WAINSDUST

Alyson puts the food back.

JAMPERDAN

Alyson gives us food.

SAM

Beautiful Alyson.

MICE *(singing in unison)*

Beeeaauuutifulll Allllyssssooon.

*(Alyson looks towards
the voices.)*

CAROLINE

Listen, Alyson, I'm—we're all worried about you. Bob,
me...Steve—all of us.

ALYSON

I'm fine, actually. I've been working from home.

CAROLINE

That explains all the mess...

ALYSON

Well, I've been busy.

CAROLINE

Well, let me help.

ALYSON

I'm good.

CAROLINE

You won't let me help you clean up?

ALYSON

Oh. It's still good. See?

> *(She opens one of the*
> *boxes and begins eating*
> *the food.)*

WAINSDUST

She's eating!

JAMPERDAN

She's eating!

SAM

The food nourishes her.

JAMPERDAN

As the food nourishes us.

ALYSON

See?

CAROLINE
This one had... mouse turds in it.

*(ALYSON looks down.
Spits the food back into
the container.)*

WAINSDUST
She has found our garden!

SAM
She does not worship it.

JAMPERDAN
Why does she spit?

CAROLINE
Are you going to throw that out?

ALYSON
No...

CAROLINE
Why not?

(pause)

ALYSON
I can't go to the museum today.

CAROLINE
Ally...you need to get out...

ALYSON

Go ahead.

CAROLINE

We had a name for him you know. The Penishead. It's what we called him.

ALYSON

Wow. Thanks. I'm all better now. You're amazing. You should start your own talk show.

JAMPERDAN

Who are they speaking of?

WAINSDUST

The Fighter.

CAROLINE

He used you.

ALYSON

He wants me back.

WAINSDUST

He shoved Alyson.

JAMPERDAN

Shoved her.

SAM

Shoved her.

WAINSDUST

And he took the green papers out of the big bag.

ALYSON

Shut the fuck up! JESUS CHRIST just shut the fuck up! Everybody shut the fuck up!

>   *(Alyson picks up a
>   container and throws it
>   at Caroline.)*

CAROLINE

Okay. Okay. I'm leaving.

>   *(Alyson picks up the
>   container, opens the
>   lid and looks down
>   at it. She throws it on
>   the floor. She grabs the
>   prescription and sits at
>   the table and stares at
>   it.)*

JAMPERDAN

She worships the plastic cylinder.

WAINSDUST

And the tablets inside.

SAM

Perhaps it was because she was shoved.

WAINSDUST

By the Fighter.

JAMPERDAN

She was shoved by the fighter.

SAM

The tablets killed Mertagale.

JAMPERDAN

Mertagale is dead.

WAINSDUST

Mertagale.

ALL 3 IN UNISON

Meeeeertagaaaaaale.

ALYSON

Shut up shut up shut up SHUT UP!

> *(SAM enters. He is
> dressed smartly in a
> button down shirt and
> pressed slacks. He sits at
> the table.)*

SAM

Mertagale.

*(He takes the pills from
out her hand. Places
them back in the
container.)*

You do not want the fate of Mertagale.

JAMPERDAN & WAINSDUST

Meeeertagaaaaaaale.

ALYSON

Who... is Mertagale?

SAM

135 hours ago.

(He begins singing.)

Mertagale.   By the   stove.   He succumbed to the
tablets.

JAMPERDAN & WAINSDUST

(join in 'By the stove.')

By the stove. He succumbed to the tablets. The tablets
in the cylinder.

ALYSON

 My pills?

SAM

There on the floor. By the stove.

ALYSON

The mouse?

SAM

The mouse! It is true. The mouse Mertagale!

WAINSDUST

She knows! The mouse Mertagale! Friend of Wainsdust.

JAMPERDAN

Mertagale! Friend of Jamperdan!

ALYSON

Who are you?

SAM

Sampulambin. Friend of dead Mertagale. And Wainsdust. And Jamperdan.

ALYSON

Sam. God, you even look like him.

SAM

We cannot have you succumb to the pills.

JAMPERDAN

Then there would be no food.

WAINSDUST

We promise not to shove.

ALYSON

How did you get into my apartment?

SAM

We live here. In the walls.

(He begins singing again.)

The walls…The walls where…

JAMPERDAN & WAINSDUST
(joining in)

The walls where…

ALYSON

Please. No.

SAM
(singing)

Alyson is beautiful.... Alyson gives us food.

JAMPERDAN & WAINSDUST
(joining in)

…beautiful.... Alyson gives us food.

SAM

And there will be no more shoving. Or the yelling.

JAMPERDAN & WAINSDUST

No more shoving…yelling. We hate the yelling.

(Sam opens up a food container.)

ALYSON

Hey. Hey—no. Don't eat that.

SAM

Why?

ALYSON

It's...it's got mouse droppings in it.

SAM

That is our garden. Our present to you. We leave it in our dances. For the food.

> *(Sam begins eating again.)*

ALYSON

No! No. You can't eat that.

SAM

But it nourishes me. And soon we will be in a family way. Soon we will be together.

JAMPERDAN

Sam will sing for Alyson.

WAINSDUST

Alyson will be with Sam.

SAM
(singing)
Beautiful...beautiful Alyson. She gives us food.

JAMPERDAN & WAINSDUST

(joining in)

Beautiful Alyson. She gives us food.

SAM
(continues)

The food gives us health. And then we dance. We dance for Alyson. Alyson is beautiful.

JAMPERDAN & WAINSDUST
(also)

The food give us health. And then we dance. We dance for Alyson. Alyson is beautiful.

> *(Sam grabs Alyson's arm. She pulls away, and in the process, the pills fall on the floor.)*

ALYSON

Fuck!

> *(Alyson drops down and begins picking up The pills.)*

Fuck fuck fuck fuck fuck fuck fuck fuck....

> *(She begins crying.)*

SAM
(singing)

Alyson on the floor...

ALYSON

Stop. Please stop.

(Sam kneels down next to her.)

SAM

(He sings)

Alyson wants the pills. But she doesn't realize how beautiful she is. How beautiful… How beautiful… The beautiful, beautiful Alyson…

JAMPERDAN & WAINSDUST

(from 'how beautiful')

How beautiful… how beautiful…. The beautiful beautiful Alyson.

(Sam takes the pills from Alyson. He drops them on the floor. He takes her hands. Continues singing.)

SAM

Alyson does not need the pills. She is too beautiful.

(They dance.)

SAM

(singing)

She dances, and in her garden she is beautiful.

JAMPERDAN & WAINSDUST
(joining in)

In her garden she is beautiful.

SAM
(singing)

Beautiful, beautiful Alyson.

JAMPERDAN & WAINSDUST
(joining in)

Beautiful, beautiful Alyson.

> *(They dance for a while,*
> *Sam sings without*
> *words. JAMPERDAN*
> *& WAINSDUST join*
> *in.)*

SAM
(singing)

Beautiful, beautiful Alyson.

JAMPERDAN
(underneath, singing)

No more shoving.

WAINSDUST

No more fighting.

SAM
(singing)

She nourishes me.

> ### JAMPERDAN
> *(underneath, singing)*

No more yelling.

> ### WAINSDUST
> *(underneath, singing)*

No more shoving.

> ### SAM

We will be together always.

> ### JAMPERDAN
> *(underneath, singing)*

Always together.

> ### WAINSDUST
> *(underneath, singing)*

No more shoving.

> ### MICE
> *(in unison)*

Alyson is beautiful. Beautiful Alyson.

> *(Alyson pulls away from Sam. She turns to the table. She picks up the containers of food and begins throwing them away.)*

> ### SAM

Why do you throw away the food?

ALYSON
Because… I don't believe you.

SAM
(singing)
Beautiful...

*(Alyson puts her hand
on his mouth.)*

SAM
Yes.

(Sam exits.)

*(Alyson gathers up the
pills one by one and
puts them in the bottle.
She exits.)*

(Lights fade. We hear a snap.)

Ryan Whinnem is one of the founders of Mobtown Players in Baltimore, and its Artistic Director through seven of its nine seasons. He has written several plays, including Mouse Song *(part of WHWN's first ten-minute playwriting workshop) and* Beans and Rice. *He has a degree in writing from Johns Hopkins University and is currently a Masters candidate in Directing for Theater at the Catholic University of America.*

Gateau

Lindsay Reed

Scene: A small table. Various items to indicate a kitchen.

GIRL: A plain, but pretty girl in her late-20s, wearing glasses. She is dressed in jeans and a black shirt, wearing no make-up and her hair is pulled into a ponytail.

CAKE: A large chocolate cake in a fancy pink box tied with string. The lettering spells out "GATEAU AU CHOCOLAT." To be opened at the beginning of the play to reveal a large chocolate cake. The cake speaks from off stage in a sugary voice with a French accent.

> *(Girl enters and places the pink box on a kitchen table. Unties the string to reveal a large chocolate cake.)*

GIRL

You know, you could just call yourself "cake"?

CAKE

Would you want to eat me then? If I was just "cake"?

GIRL

Probably not.

CAKE

You wouldn't have even looked at me in the store. Never mind bought me. Who wants "cake" when they can have "gateau"?

GIRL

I don't want you. Not really.

CAKE

Mon dieu! Not again.

GIRL

What?

CAKE

You don't want me. You want love or understanding or comfort or something else. You do not want gateau!

GIRL

Actually, I was thinking that I wanted vanilla instead. Just that maybe I should've gotten vanilla.

CAKE

Oui. Vanille.

GIRL

Yeah, vanilla. You know, vanilla cake. Sometimes I just want cake. It's not that complicated.

CAKE

It's always that complicated.

GIRL

What the hell do you know about complicated? You're cake.

CAKE

I know you can't make life with just flour, sugar, and eggs. Ce n'est jamais assez. It is never enough.

GIRL

What?

CAKE

It will never be enough—assez.

GIRL

Enough of what?

CAKE

What do you care enough of what? All you want is cake.

GIRL

No offense, but I didn't buy you to get a bunch of cryptic little French comments.

CAKE

Why did you buy me then?

GIRL

For the same reason everyone buys cake. I was hungry.
I walked into the bakery, looked around and there you
were. Simple enough. Chocolate cake.

CAKE

It's gateau au chocolat.

GIRL

Fine. Gateau au chocolat. Whatever. You looked good
and I was hungry.

CAKE

But, I must ask—hungry for what? Is it your birthday?
Are you throwing une soiree? Will a handsome guest be
joining us tonight peut-etre?

GIRL

No.

CAKE

Non?

GIRL

There's no one.

CAKE

Why not?

GIRL

Listen. I don't know why there's no one. It's not my
birthday and I'm not throwing a damn soiree. It's just
you and me and the silverware.

CAKE

I am only trying to understand.

GIRL

Understand what? It's not that complicated. Cake tastes good. I wanted some. I'm not that interesting.

CAKE

You are interesting to me.

GIRL

Really?

CAKE

Oui. You are a beautiful girl, yet you are all alone tonight with an entire gateau au chocolat before you. Pourquoi?

GIRL

You think I'm beautiful?

CAKE

Of course, ma petite amie. But, also, I see that you are alone.

GIRL

But, I'm not alone my sweet gateau au chocolat. I have you.

CAKE

Of course. But, I have already explained. I am not enough. Where are your friends, your family, your lovers?

GIRL

They…They're. Listen. If you're not enough for me, than you need to just sit on my kitchen table with your mouth shut. And be a good fucking cake like all the other good little cakes in the world.

CAKE

Have you had many other cakes?

GIRL

What the hell's wrong with you?

CAKE

Pardon. I did not mean to offend. Please...

GIRL

Sorry...sorry. I'm not offended. It's just that things have been...hard lately. And I was just wanting something... some cake...

CAKE

Ma cherie, what could possibly have been so tres difficile?

GIRL

I'm just having a few bad nights. It's nothing...I'm fine.

CAKE

Nothing?

*(Girl gets a fork. Begins
eating small pieces
directly from the cake.
Continues to eat while
she speaks.)*

GIRL

Well, not nothing, exactly. I should be fine. I'll be
fine. I'm just in the middle…and I thought that some
cake…

CAKE

S'il vous plait. Go on.

GIRL

I'm getting a divorce.

CAKE

Non! Was it a tragic love affair?

GIRL

Not exactly. Not a love affair. Not anything really.

CAKE

You married a nothing really.

GIRL

Sort of.

CAKE

Je ne sais pas. I do not understand.

GIRL

Matt was safe. Easy. He wasn't going anywhere...ever.

CAKE

In life?

GIRL

No, not in life. I mean, he was a lawyer. I mean that he wasn't going anywhere from me. He would never leave me.

CAKE

So, you left him I assume.

GIRL

He would've never left me. Not ever. Even with everything...

CAKE

Never?

GIRL

I remember on our first date, I told him this story. I don't remember a lot of my childhood. Like I sort of remember parts, but I think I just remember it from a picture or something. But, I told him about this one memory of my dad. I think it's probably my first memory. *(pause)*

CAKE

What was it, ma cherie?

GIRL

It was my dad. He told me he was going to go stay with a friend. That he'd come back in a few weeks. I think I was maybe four, I think four. And I knew. *(pause)*

CAKE

You knew what?

GIRL

He was never coming back. Never. He was lying to me. We had this brown rug. I'm pretty sure my mom picked it. And I sat on the stairs screaming. I was crying and I just looked at the brown rug and…

CAKE

Did you deteste the rug?

GIRL

Probably. I was just screaming…I couldn't stop screaming. And I remember that I gave him this picture. I yelled at him to wait, to wait…and I got it for him. It was a stuffed beagle. It was all patchwork-looking, like I'd sewed him up. He still has it.

CAKE

A beagle? A chien?

GIRL

I know…it's stupid. I guess I was thinking…I guess I thought it would make him stay. My beagle drawing.

CAKE

Did your father ever return?

GIRL

Mmm...no. They divorced a few months later. But, so...
that was the story I told Matt. On our first date. And
he promised he'd never leave me. On our first date.

CAKE

Tres romantique.

GIRL

It was pathetic actually.

CAKE

He was pathetic?

GIRL

Maybe. I guess...maybe we both were.

CAKE

And you left this...this Matthieu?

GIRL

Yeah.

CAKE

But, why? He would never leave you.

GIRL

Never.

                          CAKE
Oh...I see.

                          GIRL
You do?

                          CAKE
Oui.

                          GIRL
Well, it took me five years to see. I never loved him...
not really. He was just always going to be there, like
the furniture. Like a stupid couch...not going any
damn place until I bought a new lamp or something.
Honestly, I liked our fucking couch more than him.
But, now...

                          CAKE
...it is only you. Now it is clear.

                          GIRL
What's clear?

                          CAKE
I see why you have brought me here tonight.

                          GIRL
What are you talking about?

                          CAKE
I watched you at the bakery...layered cakes, chiffon
cakes, pound cakes, gateau. You did not pick me with

your stomach. Your heart is what brought me here. But, I have told you already…I am not enough.

CENTER
GIRL

To eat? What the hell's wrong with you? I just wanted some cake. I was just talking about…about nothing.

CENTER
CAKE

And do you intend to eat me all alone in this kitchen?

CENTER
GIRL

I already told you. There's no one. It's just…

CENTER
CAKE

I know. It's just you. Only you. You are utterly alone.

CENTER
GIRL

No! Maybe there is a soiree and I'm just not telling you. Maybe…maybe we're about to carve you into tiny pieces and I'm just keeping you calm until the final seconds of your pathetic cakey-life.

CENTER
CAKE

Ma petite amie, if only that were the truth.

CENTER
GIRL

It is the truth!

CENTER
CAKE

Bien. When do the guests arrive?

GIRL

Later! Jesus Christ! Stop talking to me!

CAKE

You should be getting ready then. You cannot possibly wear that for the party.

GIRL

Shut up! I'm wearing this. It's fine. Everyone will…

CAKE

Please…calm down. You do not want your guests to see you so upset.

GIRL

What're you trying to do to me? I haven't done anything to you…you…goddamn cake.

CAKE

True. I am sorry. The outfit you have on now will be fine.

GIRL

What? Jesus!

CAKE

Look at yourself. You have no one. You have nothing. You have a goddamn cake. Don't you see? Look!

GIRL

Shut up! You're a cake. You don't know me. You don't

know what I have. I have…God damn it! Leave me alone.

CAKE

You are the one who walked into my bakery. You brought me here tonight. You made the decision to be alone and still you are terrified. I am only asking you to see what you have done.

GIRL

I already told you—I was hungry.

CAKE

Non! You were lonely.

GIRL

No. I was hungry.

CAKE

You are lying to us both.

GIRL

I was hungry.

CAKE

If that is what you believe, fine. But, you were never hungry for gateau au chocolat, for vanille layer cake, never hungry for cake at all.

GIRL

No? Then what was I hungry for gateau? What is it that I want?

CAKE

What does it matter? You will not listen to me.

GIRL

Tell me again. I promise to listen. What do I want?

CAKE

Only you can answer that question, ma cherie. But, I am quite sure—it is not cake that you want.

GIRL

You want to know what I think gateau?

CAKE

I cannot even imagine.

> *(Girl stands up and grabs a fork. Stands over gateau.)*

GIRL

I think you just don't want me to finish eating you.

CAKE

You foolish girl!

> *(Girl stabs at the cake with the fork and pulls a huge piece to her mouth. Shoves the cake in her mouth. Speaks with her mouth full of*

cake.)

GIRL

Who's the fool now, Gateau?

> *(She stares at the*
> *cake for a moment...*
> *expecting, perhaps, a*
> *pained expression.)*

CAKE

Did you think I was to say "OUCH"?

GIRL

I was hoping I'd shut you up.

CAKE

It is not possible. You know what I say is the truth. Even now...you still have nothing. You are still hungry!

GIRL

Not for long.

> *(Girl begins to devour*
> *the cake frantically.)*

CAKE

Have you had assez, enough? Is this what you wanted?

GIRL

I hate you!

                    CAKE

You cannot hate me. You don't even want me. You want
love.

                    GIRL

End it with the fucking commentary!

                    CAKE

Non!

                    GIRL

I'll shut you up.

                    CAKE

You cannot silence me.

                    GIRL

Stop talking!

                    CAKE

I'm not talking. I'm just a cake. You hear only your
own fear!

                              *(Girl violently finishes
                              off the cake. Puts cake-
                              covered hands and arms
                              down at her side.)*

                    GIRL

Just a cake?

CAKE

Yes.

GIRL

I thought...

CAKE

Yes. I know what you thought. But, you were wrong.

GIRL

It just seemed like...

CAKE

Like I could be your friend, could spend the night with you, could keep you from facing the empty chairs, the silence, the knock at the door that never comes, and the empty bed at the end of it all.

GIRL

Je suis seul.

Lindsay Reed is a high school English teacher. She enjoys baking, eating, and tending to her houseplants. She is only now starting to lose the fifteen pounds she put on while writing the play. About the play she writes, "This is an earlier version without all of the changes from the director. The idea came to me after a night of eating way too much food and being sick to my stomach. It seemed too silly until Leo (Horrigan, Revolvers, *in this anthology) read the cake part with such French brilliance that Gateau became a real character. Interestingly, on the read through, the women all understood the idea completely and the one man was totally baffled by the premise."*

Poetry

A Plastic Soldier

Mare Cromwell

Why is it that when I seek refuge
in my garden
from the subtle angst circling far,
my shovel hits a plastic soldier,
a toy from a child
who sought to win the battles of childhood
and carry a gun when he could?

I'm trying so hard to ignore
the chaos of terror that is blooming
all over the land,
to just plant my bulbs for spring
in hopes that flowers are the only thing
that will reign then,
and fear shall have crawled back into a dormant den.

I so yearn to never dig up another soldier,
or bury one,
I want to hold onto all the men who are ready
to pull on their fatigues,
and hug them so hard
they've lost sight of battle,
regardless of who they're fighting for.

I want all mothers to sleep at peace at night
knowing their sons are out planting wheat at day
in the stillness of the field,

and I may never dig up another soldier
during war,
but only bulbs that need to be divided
and replanted for more quiet joy
in the spring.

October, 2001

Dear Garden

Dear Garden,
north as you are,
you speak to me of tenderness
and healing.

Of acceptance and forgiveness,
in mullein and poppies who volunteer their love
and light,
between lettuce and beans,
and seeds from distant lands.

You speak to me of patience and nurturing—
a being of wisdom deeper
than the incarnate ones
who tend you.

A trust runs true
in the sowing of the seeds,
belief in the fruit you
give.

You emanate a compassion and stillness
that my Self absorbs
while sitting in the afternoon sun,
playing with Fattie, the cat,
who knows the love
of the pollen
and land.

June, 1995
California

Held the Ice

Have you ever held
a piece of ice, so cold
that your fingers could hold
only so long,
until you had to let go,
and drop it,
so it could melt away?

Have you ever then tried so
to pick it up and
hold it longer,
until the numbness stilled
in the palm of your hand,
and there was no feeling —
is this that barren place called
loneliness?

Does holding ice ever
eventually
bring warmth?

1996
New Hampshire

Key West Death

There is something
 about a bird,
 a dusky bird with yellow bars on its wings
        dying in front of me,
        after I scare the cat away.

Someone wrote about riding the last breath
 to meet God,
 but I see a scattering of feathers and
        body and bones crumbling
        to bare dirt in time.

The cat was feral on an island
 of transplanted people
 with lost hearts and darkened skins,
        eating their souls away on
        tourists' crusts and salt breezes.

Breezes that blow the feathers
 to palm fronded yards,
 and narrow streets and tiny homes of decadence,

and wild cats and few breaths that rise up
to meet the creator of this sordid Key.

2001
Key West

She is...

She is the woman
who married for wrong,
an amorphous jelly shape
who conformed to the shell of a bond,
viscous, soft, vulnerable,
nothing without her home.

A woman who produced springs off
her tissue, life flows
from her orifices. She slips
from breast to thrust
like a waterhole
gives to herds in drought.

She is the woman
who batters around her shell,
a rod pistoning in her head, her heart
shaking no sense, rattling a
million obligations to a father/
son/husband on the dollar bill.

She strains to take the calcium

to keep her shell strong
and absorb the resilience
into a form that can glide
with grace
to carry her dreams out the door.

Lurking in the shadow
of suburbia, she waits
for the moon to fill,
her blood to surge,
and the call of her sisters to
touch the sacred sea.

A woman, she is a woman,
who yearns to hear,
to rise to the sound
of the waves pound, but instead
listens for the man to come
home with the kill she cleans.

1997

Not a Pew

the pew could not hold me
captive in musty stain-glassed
colors that don't match my calling

sunday morning yearns deeply
to stride my limbs

in the woods so that I may hear Creator
as a hawk

crying to me to see
with vision beyond eyes
the muffled wisdom of ancient hills
which echo peace in silence

the mother of millennia
settles into my heart as I touch a fallen bud
from an arching cathedral of trees

I have found my god and goddess
and they are not in a book nor from your tongue
they are joy surging through
my center speaking bliss

in return my very spirit sings
in the body I walk in gifted from Earth
as the hawk cries calling me to remember
that we are all divine
a song no pew could hold

2001

Mare Cromwell is the Director of Sacred Dog Productions. She is a sustainability specialist and author of If I Gave You God's Phone Number…Searching for Spirituality in America. *With a Masters in Natural Resources from the University of Michigan, she has worked in the environmental field for twenty-six years both internationally and locally in the Baltimore-Washington region. Most recently, Mare was the Executive Director of the Prettyboy Watershed Alliance. She has led dozens of sustainability workshops in the Mid-Atlantic region.*

Write Here, Write Now

Fiction

One Last Hit

Eric Goodman

Charlie hovered at the back of the train's passenger car, watching the people in their seats. There was one person in particular Charlie wanted to keep his eye on: Gene Silverman. Silverman was an easy man to keep in sight; the whiz kid rose tall above the crowd with his crown of silver hair. Charlie walked past him and found his own seat, but continued to scan the car as a pretense for keeping his eye on his target.

Charlie was an observer by nature, so tuned in to those around him that he studied them even when he wasn't thinking about it. By habit, not by nature, he corrected himself. After all, what was a person's nature if not an internalized skill or habit? People-watching was a necessary skill in Charlie's line of work, one he'd been forced to learn. Now, it had become second nature.

He had until Chicago to do the job. He needed to keep Silverman in sight for the bulk of the trip. He'd wait until the rural flatlands of Indiana to confront him.

With the train flowing steadily along—choo-ka, choo-ka, choo-ka—and with most of the passengers settled in for the long ride ahead, Charlie once again leaned forward and peeked around discretely, looking at all the people he didn't care about in order to steal a glance at the one he did. Silverman sat with a yellow pad of paper open on his lap. Charlie stood up and walked past him, returning to the back of the car. He took a pack of non-filtered Basics from the pocket of his brown leather jacket and flicked his wrist until one of the cigarettes popped up. He took it into his lips, returned the package to his pocket and got out his gold Zippo. With a practiced, one-hand motion, he sparked fire.

An old man seemed to appear out of nowhere. "Hold it, there, Mister." He wore a uniform with the Amtrak name and insignia on the shirt. "I'm afraid there's no smoking on the train."

"No smoking?" His voice was as rough as his appearance: purposeful, intense, demanding. "You mean to tell me I can't even have a cigarette here in back?"

"Afraid not," the old man said. "Company policy. Now, you can get off and smoke at the stations on the platforms if you'd like. But not on the train. We're a smoke-free train."

"Ain't that something," Charlie griped. He put the cigarette back in the pack and walked slowly to his seat. Moments later, he peered back again. Silverman still stared at his yellow pad with blank eyes, not seeming to read it. *He ain't going nowhere. If he does, I'll see him pass.* Charlie sank back into the undersized chair. He could allow himself to rest, but he couldn't go to sleep. He had to stay alert. When he got this job done, that would be it. He'd be out. It would be enough for him to retire on. *I can't screw this one up.*

Chapter 2

Before sending Charlie after Silverman, the Boss had filled him in. To say that the Boss had all but forgotten Eugene Beckett (aka Gene Silverman) was true enough; that is, he had not forgotten his former employee at all. It was as big a surprise as any the Boss had ever received, when he realized the whiz kid wasn't coming back—a bigger surprise than when the kid had set up their entire new enterprise with the identity theft and Internet crimes. Eugene had screwed the Boss in the ass by taking off without training a replacement. The kid had had left the Boss with an enormous system that nobody else knew how to manage. Eugene Beckett needed to be taken care of.

On the other hand, the Boss owed a lot to the kid, not the least of which was gratitude. A replacement could be found. The Boss couldn't manage the on-line bookkeeping or the accounts, but the prostitutes, drug dealing, and gambling racket still brought in the dough. It took a few weeks, but the Boss made some calls, screened some people, and found someone who could take over the kid's duties. Eugene had set them up with a great business and doubled the organization's income with little to no increased expense. Was that something to punish, especially considering that the kid decided to leave all future profits to him?

No. If anything, Eugene Beckett deserved royalties. That's why the Boss had let it go. Water under the bridge that flowed on and was replaced by more water. The Boss had practically forgotten the kid…until the little bastard resurfaced with a new identity—as Gene Silverman—with talk about legalizing the illegal activities that had made him who he was.

Gene Silverman was a cocky man with silver hair and silver-tongued words, words that advocated making drugs, gambling, and prostitution legal on a national scale, words that, if they continued to spread, could mean an end to the life the Boss and his gang knew. Silverman needed to be silenced; the Boss put some men on the job to dig up his story.

The Boss often described surprises as unexpected gifts received without occasion: a string of pearls for the skillful girls who'd known how to make him feel good; the extra wad of bills to the dealer who'd managed to move a briefcase full of coke the night before the cops were to raid the buyer's crack-house; the home theater for the nice cop who'd tipped them off. These were surprises, and the Boss liked surprises.

But there were surprises he did not like: finding out one of his prostitutes had AIDS and, desperate for money, didn't tell him but kept turning tricks, infecting several loyal customers; catching one of his men pinching from the drugs he was supposed to be selling, and stealing from the money he was getting for what he sold; the whiz kid leaving him—and to top it off, the surprise that the asshole trying to undermine his livelihood was that same kid who'd helped build it up. Gene Silverman was Eugene Beckett, his spies informed him. Whatever name the little prick went by, he had to be stopped. So the Boss called Charlie.

Chapter 3

Charlie got the call in the summer, when the Boss knew he was in town to visit his teenage son. Charlie had split with his woman, but he still spent a week or so with her and the kid every few months, for the boy's sake. While Charlie was in Baltimore, the Boss invited him to dinner in the Little Italy restaurant. The meal had been good, but he'd hardly enjoyed it, anticipating what the Boss wanted. Charlie wasn't a regular employee anymore. He was a consultant, so to speak, an on-call specialist and old friend. Featured on the Boss's short list, he got summoned half a dozen times a year. But his jobs were big ones, and he was paid better for his work than most of the stooges who kept regular hours.

Charlie ate his pasta alfredo and the Boss ate his gnocchi. They drank house sangrias and talked about the Ravens and the Orioles, about Bush and Kerry, about their friends and relations. All the while, Charlie wondered what the job would be, how big, and how much. Will it be enough to get out for good? On the other hand, he didn't want it to be too big. He didn't care much for those jobs.

Most people in the area who knew the Boss also knew the Boss's business, or they knew enough not to ask. But there were those innocents who did ask, not to catch him in the act, but out of sincere curiosity. For that reason, he'd acquired one of the Italian restaurants in neighboring Little Italy and a bar in Fells Point. He still had the base at the Fells Point rowhouse, but with the new properties, he often preferred to meet people and do business in the offices of his more respectable establishments.

After dinner, they retired to the upstairs office. The Boss offered Charlie a Cuban and poured them each a snifter of French brandy, then took a seat in the leather high back chair behind his large, cherry wood desk. Charlie sat in one of the leather chairs on the opposite side of the desk.

The Boss leaned back and puffed on his cigar. Charlie followed suit. In the small attic office they soon found themselves in a musty cloud of their own making. The Boss got to the point. "You heard of Gene Silverman?"

"Yes," Charlie said. "The fool who's saying everything should be legal. Trying to put the cops out of business."

The Boss studied the ash of his cigar. "Tryin' to put us out of business."

Charlie nodded. "I guess so."

"I know so," the Boss insisted. "Not that it'll ever happen. People been tryin' to legalize pot as long as I can remember and most states won't hear of it. But still, he's startin' a regular grass-roots movement. He's got to be shut up."

"Want me to scare him? Disfigure his face or something?"

"I think a little more." His eyes caught Charlie's, making direct contact for the first time since they'd climbed the stairs. Charlie knew what the Boss found in his eyes: fear and regret, the reluctance of a tired man who no longer wanted the work. Regardless, the Boss continued. "Warnin' the bastard would just... well, warn him...alert him to us, put him on guard. He knows too much; that makes him dangerous. You know who he is?"

"Nope. Don't know his history."

"His history's with us." The deep lines of his face seemed larger in the dim light of the stained-glass lamp. "Eugene Beckett."

Charlie searched his memory. "The computer geek?"

He tried to remember the whiz kid, tried to picture him, before and after.

"The identity thief's gone and stolen himself an identity and didn't have the brains to keep it quiet. You'll silence him, but it'll take more than duct tape, I think."

"You know I've been trying to quit," Charlie said. "I'm getting too old for this sort of thing. Let's just beat him around a little. Scare him."

"Shit, Charlie. You're as good as they come. Too old my ass."

Charlie's cigar had died out. "That's just it. I've had my share of close calls with vengeful friends and clever cops. I'm getting Social Security, for Christ's sake, from the few odd jobs that I paid taxes on. I don't want to spend the last decade of my life in jail. The stakes have gotten too high. I don't want to lose my autumn years, my retirement. I've been enjoying it too much."

The Boss stared Charlie down. "This is more than just a job. It's personal. Your retirement's at risk if you don't snuff him out."

Confused, Charlie asked, "How's that?"

"Think about who we're talkin' about here. Computer whiz, identity expert. Don't you think he took some insurance when he left?"

"I don't get you."

"Silverman's got our numbers. I'll bet he's got our Social Security numbers and all kinds of incriminating info on us. He had access to everything on our computers and I'll bet he still has it socked away. If he goes to the cops, retirement's over."

The phone rang. The Boss picked up the black receiver and swiveled around so all Charlie could see of him was the back of the leather chair and the smoke rising from it. Charlie wanted out, but the money kept him in. And now, on top of that, the idea that the whiz kid had something hanging over him. How many times had he promised himself this would be the last man he would hurt or kill?

For the past few years, most of the jobs he'd been given were simple ones: he'd followed people, frightened them into paying, beaten them into submission. He'd broken a leg, flattened a nose, cracked a few ribs. He'd sliced a guy's little finger off with his cigar cutter. He didn't pretend they were good jobs, but they were better than death. He'd only taken one big job during the past year. He'd already killed enough men in his life. When he was young, death didn't bother him. Now it did.

The Boss turned around and put the phone back in the cradle, then refreshed their brandies. "Where were we?"

"You were just telling me that if I promise to do a good job on this one, it'll be the last time you ask." A tremor rang in Charlie's usually confident voice as he dared to speak so candidly to the Boss.

The Boss smiled. "You'll be paid well." He noticed Charlie's cigar was out and passed him the desk lighter. "Fifty thousand."

Charlie stalled. He flicked the lighter to life. "Since this will be my retirement bash, how about a little extra?" He puffed at his cigar until satisfied with the red-hot tip.

"Don't I always give you a bonus?"

Charlie nodded. "You do."

"I appreciate your work. You're one of the best, and I'll miss having you on call. But I understand. You've earned your retirement. You gonna get that place in the Keys?"

"Yes," Charlie answered. "And I'll keep the place here, too, for the boy and his ma."

"I hope you'll stop by and see me when you're in town."

"No doubt about it."

The Boss nodded. Silence mixed with the smoke. The Boss finished his brandy. "You do a good job, untraceable, and your bonus'll be another fifty."

A hundred thousand! With the million-plus he had saved in the bank, that would have him sitting pretty. Charlie grinned. "Hell, I'll kill his mother too."

The Boss laughed. "Not necessary," he said. "But as for Gene Silverman …" He jabbed his cigar into the ashtray, twisting it until the smoke faded.

"Consider it done." Charlie put out his own, less dramatically.

The Boss picked up the brandy bottle, almost empty. "Let me hit you with this one last time." A shared drink was the only contract they'd ever required. They raised their glasses and sealed the deal.

Chapter 4

Charlie wasn't born into organized crime; he'd sought it out. As the only child of a family living in a Little Italy rowhouse, he wasn't poor, but he'd had relatively humble beginnings that pointed to him becoming the manager of an ethnic grocery store or dry cleaner. His father was Italian and his mother was an immigrant from the Soviet Union. Some weeks they went to the Catholic church in town, other times they ventured out to the Russian Orthodox church on Eastern Avenue. They were pretty much the same, as Charlie saw it. Some of the saints were different, but they taught him the same core values: it didn't matter who you were or what you did—one church or another, one line of work or another, one ethnicity or another—life was all pretty much what you made of it. He decided early on to make his own way, and to make it big.

He started small. He got the idea when he was barely a teenager. Mid-summer days were long and pointless and even the promise of school seemed a welcome vacation from idleness. He spent his days roaming through the streets of Federal Hill—the other side of the Harbor where people had money. On a telephone pole he saw a flyer with the picture of an ugly pug, contact information, and a reward amount: $100. Back then, that was a lot of money—more than Charlie'd ever seen. He spent the better part of the next few days playing pet detective, searching between row houses, in the parks, along the streets and in the alleyways. On the third day of his search, he surprised himself when, by luck more than skill, he discovered the bulldog tied to a post outside one of the pubs along Charles Street. He unhitched it and ran to the first payphone he could find—the one in front of Cross Street Market.

"I found your dog," Charlie cried.

"Oh, you must have the wrong dog. We found Kooper day before yesterday."

Charlie was pissed. All the work with no payoff. He

kicked the dog and it yelped. Then, he got the idea to keep the dog and hold it for ransom.

Sure enough, in a few days new flyers replaced the old, a picture he'd not have noticed was different, but certainly new contact information. And a new amount: $200. He called the number. "I found your dog."

"You found Regan? That's just great!" The woman at the other end of the line gave their address, just a few blocks over. The dog was exchanged for the money, and as easily as that, Charlie found himself richer than he'd ever been before.

Charlie ate ice cream, took water taxis, stocked up on girlie magazines, and even conned himself some beer, whiskey, and cigarettes. The money lasted him a luxurious couple weeks; then he schemed for more. He managed to coax a collie out of the park on the hill and led it out of sight, then fit it to the leash Charlie carried with him. A few days later, he exchanged the lost dog for $150. The rewards varied from a disappointing thank you and a piece of pie to an overwhelming half-grand. By the end of summer, he had more money stashed in his sock drawer than his parents had under their mattress.

Fells Point was only a short walk from Little Italy. There was a lot of action in Fells Point with all the pubs and clubs, the Broadway Market, and the restaurants. He began hanging out in the area, when he wasn't stealing and saving rich people's pets. When the local drug dealers tried to sell to him, he offered to sell for them. His ambition met with success. Before he knew it, he was pushing more drugs at school than some of the adult dealers were selling on the street. At sixteen,

Charlie became the youngest member of the local organized crime ring—not including some of the prostitutes—and he discovered there was a lot more money in dealing drugs than pets.

In those days, he learned to read people. He could spot an undercover cop by the cool, guarded caution. He could weed out a nark by the fearful twitch. He knew the users from the curious by how quickly they took their purchases. Sometimes, when he stood along Broadway and the adjoining streets and watched proud people strutting by, he wanted to beat the shit out of them. Sometimes he did. Once, after a college kid threatened to tell the cops that his friend had tried to sell him a joint, Charlie was so enraged that he took things a little too far. Fortunately for Charlie, it was in an unpopulated alley and no one saw who'd beaten the poor kid to death. Guilt nearly drove Charlie out of the business altogether, but his ambition overshadowed his guilt.

The Boss found out—his spies were everywhere—and summoned Charlie. "You have a real talent for clean dirty work." Most of the jobs the Boss gave him were just warnings: broken limbs, smashed faces, roughing up. But there were occasional hits. Charlie found it less difficult to deal with the second time around, and by his third kill, it came easily. He was sly, quick, and quiet about his work. He taught himself not to care, not to hear the pleas or cries. It wasn't long before he'd become the Boss's hit man of choice. Charlie didn't enjoy it, but he was good at it, and the money couldn't be beat.

Years later, he went his own way. He'd had enough

of the violence and no longer wanted to be a full-time thug. He parted on good terms, still friends with the Boss. He parted with the understanding that he would still be called upon for favors—favors that, when done well, would be well compensated. And Charlie often came by when he wasn't relaxing in the Keys, just to say hi to the Boss, or just to see whether he could do a job or two for some extra cash. Sometimes he just stopped by to share a cigar or a joint.

Charlie was smoking in the Fells Point row house on Wolfe Street the day the computer geek showed up. He'd flown in for a couple weeks to spend some time with his son and had decided to drop in. They'd gone into the Boss's smoking chamber, the other office with lounge chairs and lava lamps instead of a desk and computer. In the chamber, Charlie, the Boss, and a couple of other guys from the organization passed some joints around. Charlie found something special in being part of a dope ring with his Fells Point gang; there was something intimate about it. Aside from the feeling of a woman's body next to his, it didn't get much warmer than the feeling of a joint passed from one person to another.

"I gotta go," the Boss said. "Gotta check on the girls. They oughta be out by now. Streets are filling up."

"Aw, come on, Boss," Charlie said.

"Gotta check on that whiz kid out there, too," the Boss said.

"Invite him in," one of the brotherhood said.

"I don't think it's his thing," the other said. They all laughed.

"Not yet, anyway," the Boss said.

"One last hit," Charlie offered, pushing the joint in their host's direction.

"The problem is, it's never the last hit," the Boss said. "It's always supposed to be the last one, but it never is unless you make it." He opened the door, letting out a puff of smoke that smelled greener than it looked.

Chapter 5

On the train, Charlie wanted to sleep, but he didn't allow it. Intuitively he looked back at Silverman; his internal clock was tuned in to his environment. The whiz kid had put away his paper and was snapping the latches of his briefcase securely shut. Then he stood and walked toward the front of the car. Charlie turned discretely around and leaned back in his seat. He watched as Silverman passed him and exited the car.

Charlie stood and followed him. As he entered the next passenger car, Silverman was exiting. Charlie hung back so as not to be seen. Finally, he watched his target enter the lounge car. Charlie stalled, buffering their entries with time.

He took out a Basic, placing the cigarette between his lips as he glanced across the car at the faces in the crowd. A few mumbles and looks from the passengers reminded him: no smoking. He grumbled and placed the cigarette behind his ear.

Charlie entered the lounge car—more than half full already, and the day was young. On one of his better days, out in the Keys, Charlie wouldn't even be out of bed yet. Silverman sat toward the center of the car with a cup of hot tea and his yellow legal pad. For a moment their eyes locked and Charlie feared the kid might actually have recognized him. *No. The few times we saw each other he was too scared to notice anyone.* Charlie let the moment of eye contact slide away and scanned the room. He didn't care about these other people, but looked at each in turn in order to make his examination of Silverman seem without intent.

He spotted a man about his age going through a leather-bound planner, a German couple drinking tea and beer, a young couple silently sipping bottled water, an Army guy staring out the window, an old woman who looked like she had one foot in the grave.

Charlie ordered a black coffee, though he wanted a cigarette and a shot of bourbon. Too early to get sloppy; coffee'll have to do. At the next stop he wanted to get off the train and smoke a cigarette, but he knew he had to stay right here with his target.

He'd wait awhile before striking. He'd wait for the rural flatlands of middle Indiana. Then he could get off in Chicago before anyone even found the body. One last hit, then there'd be no more violence.

From his seat in the corner, offering him a view of the entire lounge car, Charlie continued studying people to pass the time. He watched the gray-haired man making notes in his planner, considering them, making more notes. Another man came in escorting a retard. In time, a young man entered, jotting lines in a spiral notebook, and a woman sat with tearful eyes reading a paper she kept taking in and out of her purse. A woman with a tattoo decorating her lower back looked slutty enough to work for the Boss.

Charlie watched these people, all in their own little worlds, some of them intermingling, others completely isolated and unaware of their traveling companions, unaware of him and his intruding eyes. Charlie wondered where they came from and where they were headed. Most people went through life clueless. They had no idea they were being watched, scrutinized, whether by a guy like him or a con man, a telemarketer, or a boss. Most people were oblivious to dangers all around them. But that wasn't Charlie's concern. Only one destiny concerned him. Silverman had to die before this train reached Chicago.

Eric D. Goodman is a full-time writer and editor. His work has been published in the Washington Post, The Baltimore Review, To Be Read Aloud, On Stage Magazine, Travel Insights, Coloquio, Neck of My Guitar, *and* The Federal Voice. *He received an honorable mention in* The Baltimore Review's *2005 fiction competition. In addition to "Write Here, Write Now," Eric is involved with CityLit Project, Creative Alliance, The Writers' Center, and Maryland Writers' Association. Eric seeks an agent for TRACKS, his novel in stories (www.train-tracks.blogspot.com). Visit Eric's weblog for readers and writers at www.writeful.blogspot.com. About this story, Eric says, "While 'One Last Hit' is intended to stand alone, it's also part of a larger narrative. In the book, Charlie steers one other story, and Eugene Beckett, aka Gene Silverman, is the main character of two stories. While most of the stories in TRACKS deal with situations we can all relate to, these four stories were intended to add a little extra suspense."*

Safe Haven

Judy Turner

Frozen in disbelief, Sarah Davis shuddered, afraid to blink. She felt her mouth move frantically with silent words, but none passed through her quivering lips.

Clothespins dropped from her lifeless fingers. She watched in horror as a black specter, riding a monster of the night, bore down on her. The bike and the rider missed her by mere inches, and then plowed into the pole. At first she thought she was having a nightmare, but it was broad daylight and she was standing outside in the warm sun. Sheets billowed in the aftermath and settled to the ground, effectively covering the evidence of her terror.

Silence filled the air.

She breathed a sigh of relief as the feeling came back to her numbed body. Daniel's voice reached her ears. "Mom, you all right? You're not hurt, are you?"

From the corner of her eye she glimpsed Daniel running to her side. She assured her lanky fourteen-year-old son with a pat on his arm, "Yes, I'm fine, but I'm not so sure about our intrusive visitor."

Pulling Daniel along with her, they rushed to a moving heap of now dirty clothes.

"Did you see that awesome bike, Mom? I bet it's a Harley." Daniel's usually sullen face brightened with animation, his dark brown eyes gleaming.

Sarah could have cared less about Harleys. She was more concerned with the person pinned under the bike's weight. A string of offensive words, the likes of which she'd never heard in the Lancaster, Pennsylvania Amish community, spewed from the stranger.

Heat flushed her face. She was too embarrassed to look at her son.

"Mom, I'll pull the pole to the side while you take care of the clothes."

"If this is one of your friends, Daniel, I'll wash his mouth out with soap."

A deep, mature voice responded. "Good thing for both of us I'm not a friend."

Startled by the growling voice, she jumped back and caught her foot on the exposed handlebars. Sarah lost her balance and slammed forward onto a hard chest. Her breath whooshed past her lips with the impact.

"Be still, woman. Are you trying to kill me?"

Strong arms grabbed her, and hot breath brushed her ear. She struggled and the grip on her waist tightened.

As Daniel pulled the sheets away, Sarah stilled and watched the stranger remove his helmet. She stared into gunmetal blue eyes, shaded with thick black lashes. The absolute beauty of the rich bronze-toned skin covering finely chiseled cheekbones immobilized her. Every feature was carved to perfection. His thin upper lip, and full lower one, curved upward on one side, giving him a devilish appearance. And that's probably who he was…The Devil. And here she was lying on top of him. She had to get up. It was sinful—absolutely sinful!

She pushed on his broad chest trying to get to her feet. A few more choice words escaped his lips and she knew the blush covered her from head to toe, not only from his language, but because she noticed a pair of her white cotton panties draped on his broad shoulders.

Her heavy braid, loosened by the fall, lost its precarious hold on the top of her head and swung free. With a whack it struck the man right across his mouth. Her eyes narrowed at the amusement evident on his sinful lips. Her body jolted into a flurry of activity. It was not easy to disengage herself from him. His elbow poked the side of her breast and her temper flared to cover her embarrassment. Gaining her feet, she snatched her panties, which were now hanging from his ear, and balled them up to hide in her hand behind her back.

"You son-of-a-gun. You think this is funny."

Daniel's giggle reminded her that an impressionable young teenager stood nearby. She put a tight rein on her temper. Jaw clenched, she rounded on the stranger. "They say that people use a lot of vulgar words because they lack the education for a decent vocabulary."

"Give me a break, lady."

Sarah bit her bottom lip with her teeth, and watched him stretch his muscular arms and legs as if to test their strength against the weight of the motorcycle. She pondered the thought of those strong arms clasping her tightly just a few moments ago and butterflies erupted in her stomach.

"Hey mister, you gonna be all right?" Daniel asked.

"How the hell should I know, kid? I've never nearly been decapitated by a clothesline," he groaned, "or emasculated by a well-placed knee to the groin."

His words sank in, and a haze of red fury fired in Sarah's eyes.

"Hey mom, what's he mean emas…cu…what?"

Sarah tempered her rage to a hot simmer. "Never

mind, Daniel."

Staring straight into the man's eyes, she said, "I doubt he knows the meaning of the word either."

James let her comment go. In all of his life, he'd never met a female who could turn hot and cold on and off as if she were a light switch. Her quick temper, explosive like a firecracker, took his breath away.

The embarrassment she suffered when he saw her underwear left her looking wounded and vulnerable. Seeing her like that stirred something inside of him. Strange sensations wove their way through his mind and body.

As irritated as he was, James wanted to reach out and take hold of the warmth and cloak himself in it.

"Do you think you and the kid could help me get out from under this bike?"

"Oh, of course," she said, her voice suddenly contrite, as if she'd forgotten her manners.

He spit out instructions like a drill sergeant and soon had the two of them grunting and groaning under the weight of the heavy motorcycle. He was finally free, and he stood up to test the ankle that had been trapped beneath the bike. His eyes boldly searched her face. She appeared wary now. He could see it in her eyes, speckled with bits of gold, and framed with long, spiky lashes. Her face flushed pink, and her small straight nose lifted in the air.

Long hair, the color of a palomino's mane, a horse he'd once coveted as a boy, was partially braided and cascaded over her shoulder. Loose tendrils framed her face. His eyes traveled down her tall slender figure not overlooking the generous thrust of her chest. He already knew he could span her tiny waist with his hands. His heated gaze slid back up her body. He watched her tongue slip out to lick her lower lip, capturing his attention, and his fingers began to tingle.

"Mr. whoever-you-are, with the dirty mouth and insolent eyes, how dare you?" She stomped the ground with her small foot, and dug fisted hands into her waist.

Stretching to his full height, he blocked out the sun with his body and forced her to stand in his shadow. She immediately thrust out her chin and glared at him. His size intimidated most people, but she didn't give an inch. He admired her bravado. Only the slight quiver of her lower lip gave away her true feelings.

James knew a challenge when he heard one. This lady had guts, but his intention wasn't to anger or frighten her further, so he stepped back and looked toward the young boy, now balancing his bike upright.

"What's your name, kid?" James asked.

"Daniel," the boy murmured absently, his attention still centered on the motorcycle.

James focused on the woman. Her small teeth still worried her lower lip, and her hands twisted in her apron, still trying to hide her panties. God, she was beautiful all riled up. He moved closer and watched her eyes widen in alarm. He grinned. He couldn't help it. He grabbed the hand still occupied with her underwear and bent low to kiss it. When he heard her sharp intake of breath, he straightened up and released her fisted fingers, keeping the article of clothing.

He executed a bow. "James O'Malley, at your service," he said. He heard the bout of giggling behind him. James tilted his head toward the boy and winked. He watched color suffuse her striking face and he was once again delighted with the sparks flying in his direction.

"Now, milady, I've introduced myself. Tell me your name and I won't…" waving her white cotton panties in front of her face, "mention your unmentionables."

Tears gathered in her eyes and her lower lip trembled. James, immediately sorry he'd pushed her so far, heard the boy's hushed voice behind him.

"Oh, you're in trouble now, man."

How could James have known the tears threatening to fall were a sign to take cover? On its last pass beneath her nose she snatched the apparel from his hand. She spat out her indignation quicker than he could blink an eye, and he felt as if he had waved a red flag in front of a bull.

"Oh, oh, you arrogant, insufferable…"

"Mom, listen! This is…"

"…hind quarters of a pig, just who do you think…"

Daniel reached out and grabbed her arm. "This is James O'Malley, Aunt Hester's great-nephew."

The passion behind Sarah's tirade sputtered and died, just like his motorcycle. Her shoulders sagged and her words carried on a rush of breath. "No, you can't be!"

She perused him from head to toe.

Sliding his hands into his pockets, attempting a casual air, James grinned. "Hind quarters of a pig? Is that the best you can do?"

Her hand flew to cover her mouth as if she could force the words back where they came from. "I can't believe I said that."

This is unbelievable. The woman was mortified at her behavior; it took everything in him not to laugh. He'd been called so much worse in his life. Words as sharp as a razor blade, words that could cut deep and threaten to leave gaping wounds if you weren't tough enough. So he had learned to be tough.

"I know I don't bear much family resemblance. Are we kissing cousins?"

"Oh, brother," Daniel muttered.

"We are not cousins. So you can just take your kissing elsewhere, Mr. O'Malley."

"Well then, who the hell are you?"

"My name is Sarah Davis, Daniel's mother, and we live here with Hester. And tell me something Mr. O'Malley, would it be so difficult for you to express yourself without using profanity?"

Only one word of her tirade registered—mother, and his jaw clenched. It figures. Disappointment settled in his gut. When he first looked into her eyes, he thought, oh damn, it didn't matter what he thought. Miss-'Prim-and-Proper' wasn't for him. If her attitude was anything to go by, she was definitely not in the mainstream of life.

James rubbed the tight muscles in his neck and then held out his hand to shake Daniel's. He was surprised by the boy's strong grip. He didn't extend the gesture to Mistress Davis. Her stance was rigid, and she looked as if she wanted to throttle him with something. She had eyes that could make a man go wild when filled with sparks of anger, as they were now, or he imagined they could lure a man beyond the gates of heaven, when filled with passion.

Her hands were bunching her apron, drawing attention to the ring-less finger on her left hand.

"And where is Mr. Davis?"

James heard the gasp from her son and turned toward him. Daniel's grip on the handlebars of his bike tightened, turning his knuckles white. The color drained from the kid's face and he instantly regretted his words.

"That's a good question," Daniel whispered.

Pride and determination shone in Sarah's face when she searched her son's eyes for understanding.

Daniel released his hold on the bike and turned tortured eyes to James, who just managed to grab the bike as it made its second descent to the ground. He stood by feeling helpless, while he watched the boy run up the drive, heels kicking up gravel as he raced around the other side of the house.

Once again his arrogance got him in trouble. His curiosity was piqued. He had no business asking that question. He stood his motorcycle and walked toward Sarah. Despite her look daring him to comment, she brought her trembling lips under control.

"Ms. Davis, I'm sorry. I didn't know the question would upset anyone."

He wanted to reach out, gather her in his arms, absorb the pain he'd caused her with his query. He saw traces of it in her eyes, but by the time he reached her, it was gone. Her stiff upper lip was back.

"Excuse me, I need to go after my son."

"I don't know what's going on, but maybe the boy needs time to himself."

"Time doesn't have anything to do with it." She started to walk away and James followed close behind.

"Are you going to answer his question?"

"It's a personal matter and I have no wish to discuss it."

"Maybe we should start over."

"Look, Mr. O'Malley, can this wait until after I find Daniel?"

"I saw him go into the barn."

Sarah stopped, whirled around, surprise evident in her face.

"Give him time to calm down. Give yourself some time too."

Her eyes darted between him and the barn, and James wasn't sure which one was going to win out. She glanced again at the barn, nibbling her lower lip. "Perhaps you're right."

"I would imagine raising a teenage boy without a father could be complicated."

"Yes, it can be, among other things." James took the hand she offered. "Please call me Sarah. Your Aunt Hester will be happy you've come home." A sweet smile curved her lips at the mention of his aunt.

He held her hand in his, stroking his thumb over the calluses on the surface of her palm, enjoying her touch. Enjoying it too much. The texture of her skin excited him and he wanted to feel more than just her hand.

"Not home. I've just come for a visit."

But the pleasure ended too quickly when she snatched her hand back and her voice rose in alarm.

"What do you mean, visit?"

"I plan on staying a couple of days."

"Didn't George Martin find you?"

"Yes, your private investigator found me. Or, maybe I should say I let him find me."

"Why didn't he tell us?"

"You'll have to ask him."

James had grown tired of the private investigator dogging his every step, so he'd decided a confrontation was in order. It had only been two weeks since he'd met George Martin, the man hired by his aunt to find him and convince him to come home. James wouldn't commit to anything. He resented the private eye; it surprised him that the man chose to keep their meeting a secret. There was little doubt in his mind that George wanted to spare the old lady any disappointment. The grudging respect he felt for Martin raised another notch, because of the man's compassion. Apparently, he was a friend of the family as well.

"But George was to explain to you why it was so important to Hester. A brief visit was not her intention."

"He explained the circumstances of Hester's health, if that's what you mean."

"Then you must not understand. You're supposed to be home to stay. Your grandfather's last wish…"

"I'll use your line. 'It's personal and I don't want to discuss it.'"

"Hester needs you. If you don't plan on staying, then it would be better if she never knew you were here. It would break her heart to see you walk away after all the years she spent having George search for you. It would be cruel to leave so soon."

He couldn't give in to her plea for him to stay, no matter how passionate it was. She was fiercely protective of his aunt. Why? Who was she? How did she fit in?

His grandfather had known where he was for years— long, lonely years for a young boy—years filled with poverty and hopelessness. James would never admit to how long he had hoped and dreamed…and waited.

He definitely didn't want to talk about a wish from some old man; a wish that a small, lonely boy depended on to come true. A promise never kept. No enlightenment could possibly explain away the waiting and the belief that his 'white' grandfather would come back for him. He didn't want to hear it.

"I don't stay anywhere too long. I like to move around."

"But, this is your home."

"You can't miss what you never had." James glanced around the property; his eyes settled on the old clapboard house with the wrap-around porch. The house looked lived-in and loved. Tossing these crazy thoughts aside he turned back to Sarah. The signs of distress and sympathy in her eyes angered him. Pity was the last thing he wanted from her.

"You'd be surprised how many people do very well on their own. Family and hearth is probably not all it's cracked up to be."

Glancing away from Sarah, James saw an old woman cautiously making her way down the front steps of the house.

"Is that my aunt?"

"Oh, no! Hester, you can't do that." After the fast sprint across the yard, Sarah had difficulty catching her breath. "You could have tripped and hurt yourself."

Hester's hands were now extended and Sarah gazed at the look of rapture on her face. Feeling James's presence right beside her, Sarah moved to grasp Hester's arms, but realized the spread hands were not meant for her, but for James. Hester's watery blue eyes never left her great-nephew's face.

Before she stepped back to allow Hester to receive her nephew, giving them the privacy they needed, Sarah squeezed his arm in warning, along with a look that spoke volumes.

Deep inside, Sarah was happy that Hester finally had her dream realized. But not knowing James, she felt a need to protect Hester. So she moved to the side, watching to see if he heeded her warning.

She wouldn't hesitate to put her life on the line for this dear old woman. Hester had opened her arms and her home to a scared sixteen-year-old kid who had nowhere to go—a girl who had been shunned by her Amish family—a girl who was pregnant. She remembered a feeling of inner peace and contentment filling her when she crossed over the threshold of Hester O'Malley's home.

She had hoped to find work in exchange for room and board, but she found more than that. She found security and a loving home with Hester. Not once had Hester ever made Sarah feel badly about herself. Not once had she ever violated her privacy.

Hester's health was failing more and more every day. Sarah wished she could stop the clock, which endlessly ticked away. Each minute that passed took Hester away from her and Daniel, which in turn made each minute precious to them. She made a vow to protect Hester, just as Hester had protected Sarah and her secret all those years ago.

Judy Turner is currently a romance novelist (currently because she's branching into nonfiction) who, along with her co-author, Cindy Smith, has published two books, Odds Against Tomorrow *and* Safe Haven. Safe Haven *is one of five finalists in the Short Contemporary category, in The National Reader™ Choice Awards sponsored by the Oklahoma Chapter of the Romance Writers of America. Judy is currently working on a paranormal romance called "The Secret."*

Darkened Sky

Nancy O. Greene

It was crowded, dank, lonely, the kind of place that breeds contempt and a sense of entitlement without effort or knowledge. I was one of the many that clung to the shadows, watching people go by like tourists, animals, the walking dead, but unlike most, my face was forgettable—at least I had that. A bit of anonymity amongst the filth and degradation so I could move fluidly, biding my time until my sentence in that purgatory came to an end.

My father left my mother and me when I was a baby, and at that time she restarted her drug habit. Cocaine, heroin, prescription meds, Nyquil, cigarettes, weed, whatever it took to get at least a minimal high. I was five years old the first time my mother forced my lungs full of smoke and ash. Whether it was a plain cigarette or something else remains a mystery to me. There are still so many details that escape my mind, hovering only briefly, like moths catching the scent of discarded linens. Then they float away and I am left to wonder what it was I was thinking of; but that is dwelling in the past.

I stood on the corner in one of the most dangerous neighborhoods in town, keeping my eyes straight ahead, seeing what I needed to see and nothing more. A woman was crying in the alley and her sobs echoed through the dark streets, only adding to the many ghosts that went unnoticed. Her moaning would no doubt draw the attention of those that will gladly put her out of her misery. I thought of making a noise to quiet her, but that would do nothing more than drag me into her endless suffering, like an unskilled swimmer trying to save someone from drowning, and before long the sharks attracted to her cries would also make a victim of me.

Even if I had decided to help her, it was too late. He came softly, gliding like an angel of death through the streets, around the busted cars and aimless wanderers; for a moment, nerves removed his name from my memory and a cold chill ran through my spine. If I couldn't regain my composure by the time he reached me, he would undoubtedly kill me without a moment's hesitation out of fear that I might be up to something.

He stood in front of me, waiting, his hand at his waist, and I could see the handle of a gun sticking out just within his reach. I glanced down and there were the initials DS.

"Duman," I said, training my eyes on his now, trying to cover up the smell of my fear with my gaze. He smiled. I did not say his last name; I only prayed that his first was enough.

"You're growing up, little Camille. Interested in a job?" The smile never left his face; it stretched out the scar, sliding down his cheek, and I was reminded of the monstrous stories I had overheard about him, about that scar and what he did to the man that gave it to him. Now he was asking me if I wanted a job, if I wanted to become one of the many people under his rule and command, always afraid—more so than normal in this place—always looking for a back to stab in order to get a way up or a way out. How should I turn him down, I wondered, how should I do that and not get myself killed in the process? Instead of answering him directly I just shrugged, grinned, and handed him the brown bag of money.

There was a pause. His expression never changed and he made no movement towards my offering. I could feel the heat rising to my face, the blood rushing to different parts of my body, creating the need to shift my weight, to relieve pressure. My hand started to shake, and my smile began to fade.

Just as that happened, he took the package from me. "Seems a little light," he said, riffling through the contents, then, "You didn't skimp, did you?" Now the smile was gone, replaced by a hard unwavering glint in his eyes. He lowered his hands, reaching towards his gun.

"No. It's all there." For a moment I shifted my eyes to the surroundings, seeking out anyone that might be inclined to help me. There was no one—all drug addicts and criminals themselves, they would leave me to die after stealing whatever saleable items they could salvage off of my cooling body.

He saw my nervousness and laughed. "Little one, I'm not going to hurt you. I'm just messing around. Here." He reached in his pocket and pulled out the plastic container. He didn't bother concealing it—a gram of crack and some pills, I wasn't sure of the kind. The smile came back; he winked at me and looked down at my breasts.

"You really should think about your future. Pretty soon you'll be on your own, and what will you do then, work at McDonald's?" He laughed as if the idea was the funniest bit he'd ever heard, as if it was inconceivable that anyone with access to the money he could offer would ever be interested in earning a straight paycheck.

He continued to laugh as he held my gaze, the hardened look gaining intensity. There was more to his comment than that—almost a threat. I could feel it in the back of my mind—a hand grasping at pieces of the gray matter. He implied that the best option was for me to work for him, or else. Because where could I go, where could I hide on $5.15 an hour?

"Tell your mom I said hi." And without a backwards glance, he left. A few people glanced up as he passed and immediately cleared the way for him. And as if to confirm what he'd said, they cleared a path for me, too. As I made my way out of the alley, those that were alert enough to have seen us together stayed away from me. Not so much as a leering glance came my way.

She was sprawled out on the couch, her vacant eyes staring at the flickering light coming from the television screen. I don't think she noticed me come in; even when I stood in front of the television blocking the picture, she didn't blink, so I brought out the parcel, and there—a slight shift—her eyes flickered to my hand.

"Is that mine?" Her voice came out coarse, rough like sandpaper, and the lips cracked around her words. I didn't bother to answer; I just tossed the drugs at her feet and watched as she lifted her bony body, struggling as though she weighed a thousand pounds. A glance passed between us, and then she ripped her bag open, began to prepare. When I was younger, I used to watch her, fascinated by her ability to mix these things—like she was a chef cooking the most complicated meals—and by the fact that the needles didn't seem to scare her. Needles terrified me as a child, I complained and resisted doctor's visits, and while I looked defiant on the surface I was secretly ashamed of the fact that I was afraid of something so small. Now I was no longer afraid of them; they simply disgusted me.

The phone rang. I stared at it like it was a foreign object for a second before walking into the other room to answer.

"Hello?"

"Hey, Camille." Andrew's voice poured out of the phone in that laid-back drawl that was simultaneously alluring, supportive, and commanding. We weren't exactly dating, but he didn't have a girlfriend and we did spend a lot of time together; hearing his voice made my previous thoughts drop away—I was a schoolgirl, enveloped by the promise of my crush. I was searching for words yet willing myself to remain cool, as though his call meant nothing. But I didn't want to come across as too nonchalant, dissuading his interest in me. He was 18 to my 16, graduating at the end of the school year. We had discussed which college he would attend, how he would get there, and he said I was helpful in helping him decide. We still hadn't had sex and I wondered why he didn't make a move on me; it wasn't as if either of us were virgins. I kept my questions to myself though. I wasn't going to hound him like the other girls in school did, always trying to hit him up for his number or a date behind the school bleachers.

"I know it's kind of late—"

"Nine-thirty," I said, keeping my voice low and casual.

"Yeah. You have plans?"

"I just got in, but I hadn't planned on doing anything else. What's up?"

"Just wondering if you wanted to hang out, catch a movie or something."

I looked over to my mother who was already lost in her world for the night. She mumbled incoherently, but stayed rooted to the couch cushions.

"Sure."

It was crowded at the theater—too many people I knew and too many I didn't. Andrew wasn't fazed; in fact most of the people there were glad to see him. They came over, nodded, shook his hand. Small talk took up much of our time, and within a half an hour I was ready to go home. He noticed my agitation and so did some of the females that were eyeing him like he was a fresh piece of meat and they were dying of starvation. They could sense my annoyance, too—thought it was because of them. A few challenged me with their eyes but one decided to go a step farther. Why not bump into me and cause a scene, unnerve me if she could?

"Excuse you," she said as her shoulder met mine.

"You're excused," I said, looking over her head. She was dressed in something that could barely qualify as clothing, but her heels only gave her an inch or two of extra height, so I towered over her. Andrew put his arm around me.

"What movie you want to see?" he said, looking up

at the marquee, ignoring the other female.

"You need to watch where you're going, bitch."

Her determination to be noticed was evident. At the corner of my eye I could see the gathering crowd, high school people and older all looking to see the blood, hair, and words fly through the air. It would break up the monotony of the night for some people—the dinner, movie, and home crowd. Others, they were used to violence and couldn't wait to taste the blood of someone else. I tried to ignore her. I just wanted to forget where I was and enjoy a few hours without the drama, but I knew what it would come down to if she kept pushing the issue.

That's when he showed up; a phantom out of the fog, Duman glided through the crowd with a smile on his face and a bottle of beer in his hand. Security didn't give him a second glance. Andrew stiffened, and the girl that was challenging me took a step back.

"How's it going?" he said and bowed his head slightly in our direction. It was a pretense that served a clear purpose. He knew Andrew, he knew me. He didn't even glance at the girl. She looked to us and to Duman and back again; without a backwards glance she turned and rejoined her friends. A groan rose among the crowd and most of the onlookers dispersed, uttering whispers of "What was that all about?" He just smiled, lively and a little bit drunk, but nonetheless intimidating. I pushed a smile to the surface of my face, as though he were an old friend. He glanced at me.

"Andrew, I hate to pull you away from your little date here, but I need a word." Duman walked away and into the darkness of the night outside the movie theater. It was clear that Andrew would have preferred to stay right where he was; in fact he looked as though he would have preferred to have his teeth pulled than take one step towards the waiting Duman. With a sigh he looked down at me and gave an unsure grin, his crystal white teeth catching the light.

"I'll be back in a second." I didn't want him to go; I had had no idea he was involved with Duman, but it was no surprise, really. Such a small town and Duman knew just about everyone, so why wouldn't he know Andrew? I guess I had just hoped that Andrew was different, somehow able to avoid the clutches of this man that ran the town in an almost supernatural way, impervious to even the most diligent law enforcer. A man who owned people like others owned jewelry or cars. We were only friends, Andrew and I, but he was my anchor, my proof that it was possible to leave this place behind; that like him, anyone with the skills or the brains could get into a college far enough away and never look back, proof that maybe someday this place could be less than a memory for me too.

"What movie do you want to see? I'll get the tickets," I said to his retreating back.

"Whatever you want to see," he called over his shoulder. And then he was gone. I stood staring at their silhouettes, trying to imagine what they could possibly be talking about. And then I saw it; the glint of Duman's watch as he passed something into Andrew's hand. Then the glint traveled up to where Andrew's shoulder would have been and they stood there a moment longer—Duman's silhouette changed and I could only make out the rounded curve of his head. I couldn't tell if he was looking at me or away from me, but suddenly my face started to burn and sting as if from an inferno. I turned toward the marquee. It wasn't long before Andrew stood beside me, looking up at the list of movies as if nothing had changed. He didn't say anything, he didn't touch me, and I was glad for that.

The movie couldn't hold my attention. What were they talking about? What was it that he handed to Andrew; how much was he selling? I could hear the chattering all through the theater, the laugher and shouts at the screen that came from various patrons, but it was all distant echoes in the cavern of my mind, bouncing off the walls as I attempted to regain focus. Did he own Andrew? Those words came back to me now in the theater, "You should think about your future. Where are you going to work, McDonald's?" Andrew was cold beside me, unmoving, silent. He hadn't looked me in the eye since the exchange. But then, I hadn't looked at him either.

When we left the theater he drove me home in silence. The apartment I shared with my mother loomed against the darkened sky like a monster awaiting its prey, swallowing each person that entered as indifferently as the next. I sat in the passenger seat, my mind raging, racing, searching for the right words. I didn't want to offend him. He was my friend and I cared about him, but I had to know.

"So how are you paying for college?" Our eyes met and there was confusion there, a struggle. He opened his mouth but no words came out. Then, his jaw set, he turned his head and looked out of the front window at some location down the street.

"I have a scholarship."

"Enough to pay for everything?" He looked at me again. Then he hung his head, hands playing with the plastic of the steering wheel.

"I have a few things worked out. Relatives and shit like that." There was silence again. He didn't look up at me, but I couldn't look away. Finally he looked back up and started the car.

"Listen, I have to get home," he said. "I told my dad I'd be back before morning."

The bed was cool beneath me and I lay in the dark thinking about what I was going to do after I graduated high school. My mom was passed out on the couch, sleeping the dreamless sleep of someone that had given up on the world, that had given up on the hope or dream of ever having anything more than what they already had. I wanted to sleep like that, dreamless, not even a faint whisper in the cosmos, but I couldn't.

The words came back again, and I imagined myself working at a fast food restaurant, earning just enough to get by. I imagined the sweat dripping down my hair, and the late nights and the grouchy bosses. That was no kind of life, not for me. I tried to think of the alternative, but it was too much. Duman. Being one of Duman's people—and I was female, that carried even more of the unthinkable.

Andrew had already chosen. He'd be lucky if Duman let him go twenty miles away for college, much less out of state; he really didn't know what working for a man like that meant. To punctuate the thought, a siren blared in the distance and I put a pillow around my ears to shut out the intrusion. I wanted out of this place, out of the crazed lifestyle surrounding me, but how? I only had two years—if that long—to figure it out on my own. Until then…

Nancy O. Greene is author of the iUniverse Editor's Choice and Publisher's Choice award book Portraits in the Dark: A Collection of Short Stories. *Thought-provoking, entertaining, and literary, her writing ranges from horror to sci-fi to classic character-driven narratives. This collection displays the author's talent for infusing each story with a captivating, unique voice and style. She started writing at the age of nine and has a degree in Cinema (Critical Studies) with a minor in English (Creative Writing) from the University of Southern California.*

Forever, Lilith

Fernando Quijano

3:17 pm

this is the day the universe opens up to me... the day that i throw off the chains of gravity and bound around my old home. earth. california. october 12, 2006. i remember my first, but i will never forget my last. slowhand will kill me while i come, & i will go to god.

3:18pm

The first hour is the longest. Waiting. Forty five minutes in the parking lot of El Pollo Loco staring at the opposing arrows flashing on the dash of my Infiniti, onoffonoffonoff… not too late, I whisper to myself; I can go home now, start dinner, pretend nothing happened would ever happen. I look at the dashboard again; the blinking blurs. It's nothing. Just fear. But I've been waiting too long. Most of my damned existence. No longer. My desire is finally stronger than my fear. I turn off the hazards, twist the key in the ignition, and start driving towards Sacramento.

Guilt. It should be weighing me down, keeping me from achieving escape velocity, but I don't feel much of it. Two children and a husband left behind, left to fend for themselves. I can imagine the confusion when they come home hungry and expecting. Do they deserve better?

Not really. If they did, I would have provided it.

I did provide it for the past seventeen years without much complaint and gradually diminishing expectations that they would ever appreciate it. I've bottomed out.

I know what people will think too—another cruel and insensitive bitch abandoning her litter. I can already hear the cries: *But those are your children. They didn't ask to be brought into this world.* YOU are accountable for how they act. Bullshit! In the end, we all have to be accountable for ourselves. They've had everything they ever needed and most of the things they wanted. I know I'm not free of all responsibility, but I was barely the moisture in the clay that formed them. The earth itself is the problem. It comes from this society we're trapped in. Gray. Fetid. Epidemic. If I am corrupt, it's because the earth has stained me as well. I too am its waste.

Parents should be the hands that mold the clay, but we're much too busy working hard to maintain this contrived sanity we build around ourselves for even that job. We have long since passed on the responsibility to their teachers. Of course, they don't want it either.

No, usually it's our children's peers providing the indelible hand. But what guides their peers? Spongebob, Pokemon, MTV, The O.C., America's Top Model, Eminem, 50Cent. At least we have the Oprahs and Dr. Phils of the world to solve our problems in an hour minus commercials.

We start the kids off on Sesame Street and Barney while we get some dishes done, and before we realize it, Emily's skipping breakfast and having nothing but a Diet Coke for lunch so that she can try to maintain her

Olsen Twin figure. Jacob got his first tattoo last summer at some music festival in Indio. Coachette. Coachelle. Something like that. He's not even sixteen yet. My father, The Cantor, would have railed on for hours about how scarring my flesh would prevent me from being buried with the rest of the family. But coffee-stirrer figures and indelible skin art are the least of my children's problems.

Emily wanted to hang out with the "cool" girls at Brentwood during her freshman year. She started smoking pot with them. By the end of sophomore year, she was snorting Ritalin. Bumping Rit, she would tell her friends thinking the lingo would fool me, not realizing I had sources. Not even halfway through her Junior year and she was bumping Ya, cocaine.

Jack and I did what we could, put her in a twenty-eight day program and cut off the generous allowance that had financed her drug use. Little good it all did. She was so fascinated by the kids in recovery addicted to heroin, she had to try it for herself. Once out, when we wouldn't give her money, she started dragging Jacob with her with the promise that he could hook-up with some of her friends so she could mooch from his funds.

When we caught on to that and cut him off too, they came up with a new plan. They used the gas card, the only one we still let them use because it could only be used at gas stations. They maxed it out buying cartons & cartons of cigarettes at little station stores on their way to Indio. They were able to make enough selling cigarettes at the show that they could spend the whole weekend fucked up on 'shrooms & crystal meth with enough cash leftover for Jacob to get his tattoo and for Emily to get her tongue pierced.

I gave up after that fiasco, after getting the bill for their experiment in Capitalism. I realized that we'd gotten to the point that they didn't care what we thought of them—what anybody thought. Not that anyone else cared. Brentwood still takes our money.

"They'll grow out of it," Jack had said. They were just typical children testing their boundaries. Let them test their boundaries. I'm breaking mine. If they've stopped caring, why shouldn't I?

As I head onto the freeway, (I've already been on & off twice, doubting myself because we are taught to doubt ourselves from childhood) I can't help but wonder about all the events I'll miss. Emily's prom this year; Jacob's the next. Graduations. Weddings. Grandchildren. Stints in & out of rehab. Abuse. Divorces. Bitter loathing. The ever-penetrating hatred that spreads across you like a California wildfire until it consumes you and there is nothing left but scorn & ash. Maybe they can grow from my death, avoid my mistakes. Regardless, the years they'll spend in therapy, if they're smart enough to turn to therapy, won't hurt.

Will they even miss me? Think I didn't love them because I abandoned them? Blame themselves? Well screw them!

Children think all life revolves around them. That's their greatest fault—what separates them from the barely sane adults. Like early Christians, they imagine they are the preeminent Earth, the absolute center of their universe, and everything else is supposed to revolve around them. Nothing's personal, nothing's private, and parents can't have any aspect of their lives that doesn't encompass that of their children. Well damn it, this life is mine, and if they can't accept that… accept my decision…Well, I suppose they need the sudden reality of losing their mother to blow them sober. I am Copernicus, Galileo, & Newton at once, the new perspective. Evolution. I am gravity, force & friction. Let them decide.

Jesus Christ! Can't stop sobbing. Can't even get a grasp of all the shit that's going on in my head right now. The over-intellectualized byproduct of a liberal arts Berkeley education mixed with years of guilt, angst, and self-loathing. Nineteen years wasted climbing the social ladder with Jack before plummeting off the top. The twenty years before that spent living under The Cantor's shadow. Is that who I am? Or am I something else? The demon that has reemerged with SlowHand's guidance. Lilith come forth one last time to face God and demand a reckoning!

Jack. What about Jack? My dear-in-the-headlights husband. A part of me believes he loved me once. The rest of me knows that all he saw was a chance at another notch on his belt at Berkeley when he first saw me walking across the campus. I don't have many questions left regarding Jack. I know he won't miss me. I have become a burden to him of late. He will mourn, but he'll appreciate being unencumbered by my absence.

He might blame himself. After all, he was the one who, however unwittingly, showed me where to find the trails I've traveled lately—the path I am on now and will follow to its end.

Maybe one question. Could he have done anything

to prevent this? No. Postpone, maybe. He could have at least prepared himself. No, if the prick can't take care of himself, he deserves to die a death more painful than the one I have planned for myself.

We met in an auditorium at Berkeley. Ginsberg was howling, one of the last times too—rest his soul. As I walked in, I was distracted by Jack's eyes. I could feel them on me, scalpels dissecting & analyzing. It wasn't flattering, but I was intrigued. The sharpness of his eyes matched those of his face: ragged cheekbones, jutting jawline, a crooked rook of a nose. They all looked like they could cut glass, snip tin, pierce hearts.

"What's the matter? You don't like Ginsberg?" I asked as I took the empty seat next to him. He avoided my gaze when he realized I'd noticed he had been ogling me. I could see the sweat breaking through his skin, the thought that I had caught him lost in my tits setting his face aflame. He was coy. I wasn't.

"Well…" That's Jack! Hesitation & uncertainty. He plays it off as wisdom, claiming that he likes to think about how best to answer any question. Bullshit! It takes him that long just to understand the question. But he's charismatic and he hides it well. Better yet, he's used it to his advantage. He was Pre-Law back then. I was an English major, minoring in Religious Studies, with the same aspirations to write that bestseller most English majors share. It took an effort to find some common ground.

"God?" I asked.

"Sorry?"

"Do you believe in God?" I clarified. I often found the topic a useful barometer of where a relationship might go.

"Well, no. I can't say that I do. I think God is a product of the past. I like to think we live in a more enlightened time. We don't need gods to explain our mysteries; we need Louis Pasteurs and Immanuel Kants. How about you?" He didn't seem certain. Any relationship with him might prove precarious at best, I thought.

"I don't know God. But I don't think anyone can." I was certain that nothing was certain.

We dated a while, enjoying what little common ground we were able to create. The one thing we realized we shared was a sense that artists and their art, always under attack by those who understood them the least, needed to be protected in order to thrive. We figured that we had enough brains between the two of us to do something about it.

We got married after he passed the Bar. I taught English to ninth graders while he tried to establish himself in the field. After a year of marriage, I got pregnant and he got a job offer in Los Angeles doing what he was destined to do. Lawyer to the Stars. What a shame he got lost in the glare… Been blind ever since.

It didn't take long to forget that sense of idealism we had shared. I can't even imagine why we've stayed married this long. I suppose we used the children as an excuse for that too. Not true. We were both just comfortable. I was well-kept, and his house was well kept. We both wanted something different but were too afraid of change.

The dynamic was altered when I caught him having his little virtual affair. Now we're still married because there are things I know that would humiliate him if they became public. Fear no more Jack. I'm leaving and I'm taking the dirty little secrets with me.

We thrived for a while, though, enjoying the first child, the first house, the first decorator, the second car, the second child, Jack making partner, Mutual Funds & IRAs, a second house in Aspen, Living Wills & Trust Funds, Corporations & Foundations. We were worth more than most of his clients until the tech bubble burst. But we managed to survive that too. You can never run out of celebrities fucking up.

The first computer. How'd I let that slip? Emily was starting lower school at Montessori when we bought it. Jack had his laptop from the office, a monster by today's standard, but we needed one that the kids could use as we became more serious about their educations. Why not? We had it all. Life seemed perfect.

Life, by most accounts, should have been perfect. Life should be perfect, shouldn't it? I never wrote that bestseller. The ideas filtered out as fast as the children and money filtered in. It looked like my fate lay in more domestic domains. Martha Stewart became my God, and I worshipped her willingly.

Now, if I were to turn around I would go home to three days worth of dishes piled in the sink, mold feeding on the grout in my bathroom, and my mound of mulch infested with rats. Not a good thing. Martha would be very disappointed.

Unlike Martha however, I won't see the inside of a jail cell. SlowHand however.... He deserves better— better than being relegated to being my handpicked executioner followed by the rest of his life under incarceration.

Fear again. Doubt again. If I hurry, I might get back and have dinner ready before Jack gets home. Maybe I can just blame it on hormones, get a couple of family meal deals from Carl's Jr., and tell Jack I was just out running errands, doing some early Christmas shopping, finding a new therapist. He thinks I need a new therapist. That would make him happy—happier. No. There is going to be no third time. I am done turning around. I drive. As the last Los Angelic palm disappears from the rearview, I know I am never coming back.

Fernando Quijano III has been published by The Melanin Chronicles *and* Welter. *He hopes to have his novel, "Forever, Lilith," published in the near future so he can live miserably-ever-after, but richer. "Forever, Lilith" has been a labor of love ten years in the making. Inspired by real events, it tells the story of a woman so fed up with her life that she decides to end it with the help of SlowHand, her mysterious online lover. However, when she finds herself falling in love with her hand-picked executioner, she finds that dying may not be as easy as she originally imagined. You can read more about Fernando and his writing at www.blog.myspace.com/fernandoquijanoiii.*

A Member of the Force

Barbara Friedland

Jimmy lay back on his cot and thought. Parts of his life appeared before him, as vivid as a movie. He had always been lucky. And smart.

Smart remains. One of the few diversions afforded to him was to participate in an extended study about murderers. Ordinarily a married man convicted of killing his mistress would be considered too mundane for part of a five year Harvard sponsored survey.

But he had been a cop, which took a prosaic murder and made it worth the time of the professor who came down to Baltimore several weeks each year. The first thing he did was administer an IQ test. Jimmy always did well on exams. Hell, he passed the one for Sergeant first time. Some guys had to take it over and over again. Four, five times.

Everyone but Jimmy was surprised to learn that he was in the genius range. After two more attempts, the head of the study had to concede that the initial findings were accurate.

"167 and what did it get me?" The ex-cop said out loud. In the beginning, during the first three years of incarceration, Jimmy had barely spoken, and only then to his family—several members were still visiting him then. And his lawyer. Never to the guards or anyone from the prison. He was innocent and he kept saying it over and over. He knew that his attorneys didn't believe him. Hell, he'd lost that damn gamble with Buddy taking the rap for him.

After some time, and the loneliness of protective custody, he started to sing. Soon he was telling stories. He realized that he must look like the guy he used to wave to on warm nights as he sauntered into the station house. Gus was harmless and used to sit on the stone ledge fronting the building. He had animated conversations with himself, impervious to ridicule from anyone.

"Gus." Jimmy's deep baritone echoed in the cell. "Sorry I never stopped to chat."

Jimmy was probably better looking now than he was during the trial. Or even before that when girls everywhere noticed him. He was still hard and muscled, lean from disciplined, supervised work-outs. His features, sharp, masculine, had softened. As he approached his sixties, he was a handsome man, finally shedding the coarseness that had made him look common and mean.

As he lay on the cot, Jimmy thought about those three days in his life. He always put them together. Lumped them all in time. Each incident felt like he was falling off a cliff. His stomach would churn, like it did on a rollercoaster, or when an elevator jerked and descended too quickly.

He had floated through high school. Not a lot of studying and pretty decent grades. Played for the football team. A parade of girlfriends. And some he kept around just for sex. To please him. When he was a sophomore, a rich snob, two years older than him, asked him to the prom. She drove and paid. He met her father and felt his scrutiny, his derision. The old man had boxed him in, thought him common. Jimmy just smirked. He was going to fuck this man's daughter. He would make her beg him to be with her. Sure, she was pretty. But there was a line of them, all wanting him.

The prom had been great. Sue had pursued him all through her senior year. She'd even come home from college, once, sometimes twice a month, to find him and buy him things and try to please him sexually even if he was too tired from football, or other dates, to care about her.

Her given name was Suzanna. To him, she was no better than anyone from his neighborhood and he christened her a common appellation that filled her with delight. "Daddy," she would squeal. "Call me Sue."

"No Suze," was his only reply.

Once Jimmy grew bored of her, he slept with her mother. He showed that bald bastard, with the cold eyes behind the thick glasses, that he was just as good. Jimmy smirked in his jail cell at the memory.

The first time he felt like he was falling off a cliff came in his senior year. He was lying on his bed, face up with his hands folded behind his head, thinking about college. One of his harem had just left. He made certain that she was gone before his mother returned from work. Several schools wanted Jimmy, but he would probably stay local, find a place in Maryland where he could play football and have a good time. He didn't want to go far because he needed to stay a part of the old neighborhood. His built in fan club would serve him well.

He heard his mother come in. She had groceries; he heard her feet shuffle across the broken linoleum of their old kitchen. She was calling him. In the years that followed, he chose to relive that day over and over again.

At some point, he went downstairs. His mother still had her coat on and frozen food lay on the counter top. Jimmy swooped in. He decided to be charming. Putting his large arms around her frame, Jimmy squeezed tight. "Sit down Ma. Let me help." Wordlessly, he swept up the squares boxes of peas and beans, the cheap frozen meals, the containers of juice, and stuffed them into the small freezer.

"Jimmy." His mother hunched over and pulled her coat tighter. The top two buttons were missing, and she used a safety pin in their place. The dull brown wool robbed her face of any color and her complexion looked like dried mud.

Words cascaded out of her mouth. She had been injured. Disability. Couldn't work. Even with scholarships, Jimmy could not go to college. That day was the first time that he thought he was falling, pitching to earth at an alarming rate of speed.

Jimmy kicked out a chair and fell into it. He knew his mother was still talking. He couldn't hear her, only see her mouth moving in pantomime. As he relived the memory in his jail cell, his mother morphed into Tina. Except his mistress was naked. She was smoking a cigarette and laughing. Her small pot belly shook and she giggled. Pulling up from the seat, she stuck her hand out of the window to shake the ashes away. At first she complained. Jimmy pretended to listen. He nodded occasionally. Tina was tired of always having sex in a police car. She was listing the restaurants that she wanted to try. He pulled her down, pushing her to his throbbing penis, jamming her head into his groin.

And that's when he was pushed over the same cliff.

"Stop talking and do it." Jimmy was annoyed. If he wanted yammering, he could go home. Well, not for five more hours, but when his shift finally ended.

Jimmy stopped holding her and roughly backed her against the seat. She continued to talk and this time he understood her words. Tina was pregnant.

Was it instinct or fear? Maybe he was just smart enough to know that his luck had run out. Jimmy sensed, with a certainty that fossilized into a brittle despair, that Tina would not abort this one.

The final time that the earth gave way under his feet, when he felt like flailing his arms to keep from crashing, was more than twenty years ago. When the bullet from his gun passed into Tina's brain.

Barbara Friedland is co-owner of a technology consulting firm. She also teaches marketing at a local university and writes a marketing blog that often wanders into political commentary, www.adtractive.net.

Invasion of the Orb Men

Paul Lagasse

Creeger had expected Langford and Miss Mackenzie to be highly skeptical of their new assignment, but they reacted to the news with equanimity. Both of them had become used to being shunted around ATIC from project to project. Langford had even admitted to a casual curiosity about flying saucers. Creeger felt reassured; he had picked his people well.

The three of them walked to the featureless red brick building down the road from their Quonset hut office. The fresh air from the short walk purged Creeger's lungs of the tepid, fan-blown air in their sun-baked metal tube, and by the time they got to the third floor he felt sharp and prepared.

Then he opened the door to their new office.

The three of them took in the space in silence. Sagging, overloaded bookshelves lined the walls. Rows of ancient file cabinets of assorted colors and sizes stood clustered in the middle of the floor, drawers sticking open at odd angles. Empty coffee cups and stacks of old newspapers and magazines covered the large worktables. A clutch of olive-drab metal desks with chairs that lacked various components rounded out the scene. A moldy pall hung over the room.

Creeger tried the switches on the wall, but succeeded only in creating three pools of pale yellow light—one of which immediately disappeared with a fizzle and pop.

Langford cast an appraising eye over the spectacle.

"This can be your office, Len," he said, patting Creeger on the shoulder. "Congratulations."

Smiling at Langford's comment, Miss Mackenzie ventured into the gloom toward the windows on the far wall to tug the window blinds. The resulting light didn't do much for the ambience.

"Maybe this is the wrong place?" Creeger said. He checked the number on the door's frosted window and grunted. Miss Mackenzie began clearing off a space on the largest table while Langford poked thoughtfully through a file drawer.

Creeger turned to the sound of footsteps in the hall. "I'm sorry we're late," said a short, bespectacled man carrying a stuffed briefcase. Behind him was a tall, stern-looking woman with a puckered frown.

"I'm Milton Lassiter," the man said breathlessly, extending his free hand to Creeger, who shook it. "This is Eunice Barfield."

"How do you do?" said Creeger.

"Captain," Miss Barfield replied huskily through her scowl. Her grip was limp and cold.

Lassiter fussed over his materials, which he plunked down on the table corner that Miss Mackenzie cleared for him. "I had hoped to be all set up by the time you arrived," he said. "But they have me working at the other end of the base now and…" he muttered, trailing off.

At the other end, Miss Barfield looked at the table as if it was covered with bacteria.

Creeger cleared his throat. "These are my colleagues," he said, gesturing. "Carl Langford, civilian intelligence analyst. Marian Mackenzie, my secretary."

Lassiter looked up long enough to nod at them, and returned to his muttering. Miss Barfield concentrated on finding a chair that she could touch safely.

Is this performance open to members of the audience? Creeger wondered. He exchanged poker glances with Langford and Miss Mackenzie.

The moment of theater ended when Lassiter pulled out a file with a satisfied sigh and Miss Barfield finished wiping down a wooden chair. Everyone else selected from among the non-sterilized chairs.

Creeger's wobbled threateningly as he sat in it. Hold together, baby, he thought. We're almost over the target.

"General Horn asked me to brief you on Project Grudge," Lassiter began. "I'm not the person who should be doing this," he said whiningly, shaking his balding, perspiring head. "But I'll do my best." He passed around folders for Creeger, Langford, and Miss Mackenzie. Inside was a brief timeline filled with dates and acronyms. Behind that was a report marked "Project Sign—Final Report." Following that was a report titled "ESTIMATE OF THE SITUATION" and marked "TOP SECRET."

Lassiter took a deep breath and began reading from his notes. "Okay. On 24 June 1947, a civilian pilot named Kenneth Arnold is flying over the Cascades in Washington State when he reports seeing a chain of nine shiny objects flying by Mount Rainier at tremendous speed. He says that their motion reminded him of the way a saucer would bounce if it were skipped across water." He looked at his audience over the rim of his glasses. "Flying saucers are born, ladies and gentlemen."

Creeger leaned back and folded his arms, determined to enjoy this.

"In the weeks and months that follow, dozens of flying saucer sightings are reported in newspapers across the country." Flip. "Now. 7 January 1948. Fort Knox, Kentucky. Military and civilian witnesses report a flying object resembling a red-tipped ice-cream cone. Godman Air Force Base routes a flight of four Kentucky National Guard F-51 Mustang fighters to intercept the object. Flight leader Captain Thomas F. Mantell gives chase. He reports that the object is of tremendous size and appears metallic. He then reports that he is climbing in pursuit. Nothing more is heard from Captain Mantell. Several hours later the wreckage of the aircraft is found in a field with the Captain's decapitated body inside."

"Was the aircraft shot down?" Creeger asked.

Flip. "The investigation indicated that the pilot blacked out," Lassiter said. "The particular aircraft was not equipped with oxygen gear for high-altitude operations. In his eagerness, the pilot apparently forgot. In any case, following this incident, the brand-new United States Air Force decides to initiate a formal investigative program to deal with the growing wave of flying saucer sightings. Project established under jurisdiction of Intelligence Division, Air Materiel Command, Wright Field. Project is assigned the code-name 'Sign.'"

As if he had just imparted a fact of great import, Lassiter paused and looked around the room. Creeger tried to appear like he appreciated the significance.

Flipping more pages, Lassiter continued. "The mission of Project Sign is to, and I quote, 'collect, collate, and evaluate and distribute to interested government agencies and contractors all information concerning sightings and phenomena in the atmosphere which can be construed to be of concern to the national security.' Unquote," Lassiter paused. "The unofficial prevailing view among the Project Sign senior staff is that the flying saucers are not of earthly origin."

Creeger glanced around the room to gauge reactions. Langford's eyebrow was raised. Miss Mackenzie's fingers were steepled under her chin in rapt attention. Miss Barfield continued to look like, well, whatever she looked like.

Flip. "24 July 1948, 2:45 a.m., in the air over Alabama, between Mobile and Montgomery," Lassiter resumed reading. "Broken cloud cover at 6,000 feet, a bright, moonlit night. Aboard an Eastern Airlines DC-3 airliner, pilot Clarence Chiles and co-pilot John Whitted see what they believe is the exhaust trail of an Air Force jet, ahead and above. Object suddenly dives at them and passes by close on the right, then climbs rapidly and disappears into cloud. Pilot and co-pilot report the object appears to be a wingless cylinder with two rows of lighted windows and a blue glow underneath, leaving a trail of fire. Total time in sight is ten to fifteen seconds."

Creeger whistled softly. Reports from pilots, in his experience, were usually more credible than those of untrained witnesses. And this object didn't sound like any American—or Soviet—aircraft he had ever heard of. Now he was becoming intrigued.

"Following this incident," Lassiter continued, "Project Sign issues a confidential estimate of the flying saucer situation, formally suggesting that flying saucers are, in their estimate, vehicles from other worlds. The report moves quickly up the Air Force chain of command. And then moves as expeditiously back down said chain, with orders for all copies to be destroyed." Lassiter looked around the table. "If asked, your folders do not contain copies of the estimate in question," he said quietly, with a sly smile.

"In short order," Lassiter said after taking a deep breath, "Project Sign was ordered to issue its final report and cease activities. United States Air Force, Unidentified Aerial Objects, Project Sign Final Report, F-dash-TR-dash-two-two-seven-four-dash-IA, February 1949 is officially located in your file."

Creeger nodded.

"Subsequent to the Project Sign final report," Lassiter said, "Project Grudge is established based on the recommendations in that report, suggesting that, and I quote, 'future activity on this project should be carried on at the minimum level necessary to record, summarize, and evaluate the data received on future reports and to complete the specific investigations now in progress.'" Lassiter took another breath and pushed ahead. "'When and if a sufficient number of incidents are solved to indicate that these sightings do not represent a threat to the security of the Nation, the assignment of special project status to this activity could be terminated,' unquote, and future reports can be handled through routine intelligence channels." Lassiter snapped his folder shut and sat down.

There was a pause. "And?" Creeger prodded.

"And nothing," Lassiter replied, seemingly surprised. "That's it."

"That's the briefing?" asked Creeger.

"That's the briefing," said Lassiter.

Gee, handshakes all around, Creeger thought. "I think my staff and I might have some questions. Such as, what, exactly, is our assignment here, Mr. Lassiter?"

Lassiter's harried expression ratcheted up several notches. "Didn't General Horn explain that to you?"

"Only in the briefest and broadest way," Creeger said levelly.

"I'm not sure I'm qualified to explain," Lassiter said, licking his lips. "I'm just a civilian advisor...."

Creeger closed his eyes for a moment. "My understanding from General Horn," Creeger interjected, still reluctant to accept the rapidly accumulating evidence to the contrary, "is that I would be taking over a systematic investigation of a potential national security threat, with the goal of providing assessments and recommendations as to the Air Force's course of action."

"Well, it is all here in this final report," Lassiter said, pointing to the folder.

"Yeah, but level with me here, Milton," Creeger said, leaning forward and putting his elbows on the table. "A systematic investigation of a potential national security threat requires manpower. It requires tools. What do I have to work with here?"

Lassiter glanced around the room and tried to meet Creeger's eyes after the circuit. "This," he said meekly.

"This?" Creeger barely contained himself.

"All of this," Lassiter replied hopefully.

"What about personnel? Budget?" Creeger barked.

"I wouldn't know anything about that, sir," Lassiter replied obediently.

When Creeger slowly opened his eyes after ten seconds of complete silence, he was disappointed to find himself in the same shithole office.

"What was your connection with Project Sign?" Creeger asked calmly and slowly.

"I was the records manager," Lassiter said. "I coordinated the filing of new reports, tracked correspondence, typed up the reports, that sort of thing."

Creeger's eyes trolled the office, admiring the man's handiwork.

"So aside from the military officers in charge, you were the person most responsible for the day to day operation of Project Sign?" Creeger asked.

Lassiter weighed the question for a moment. "Yes," he finally said.

"And one of the tasks of Project Grudge will be to close out the incomplete investigations from Project Sign, is that correct?"

"Yes."

"These files here?"

"Most of them, yes,"

"Most of them," Creeger echoed softly. Creeger closed his eyes for only five seconds this time. Despite the screams of his professional instinct, Creeger said, "Well, Milton, it would seem that you're the most appropriate man for the job on Project Grudge as well."

Lassiter went pink, then white, shaking his head more vigorously with each shade. "No," he said, "Oh, no, I'm not assigned to this project, I'm sorry, Captain. Oh no."

Oh yes, Creeger thought, feeling particularly nasty toward this nearest convenient substitute for General Horn, which sat perspiring and quivering before him like a sacrificial animal. Langford broke out in a wide grin.

"Miss Barfield," Creeger turned to face the other end of the table. "You were Mr. Lassiter's administrative assistant on this project?"

Miss Barfield hesitated for a fraction of a second before nodding. "Yes, I was," she said levelly.

"Well, I would value having your expertise on this project as well," Creeger said with velvety smoothness.

"Yes, Captain," she replied. Creeger hoped she didn't play poker.

Creeger stood up and adjusted his tunic. He extended his hand to Lassiter. "Welcome aboard, Milton," Creeger said, his voice precisely three shades too loud.

Lassiter bumbled to his feet and shook Creeger's firm hand weakly. "Y-yes, Captain," he said, as the others stood and gathered their folders.

"Call me Len, Milton," he said, slapping Lassiter's shoulder. "Or do you prefer Milt?"

"Er…" Lassiter said, clearly preferring neither. "Milton is fine," he said.

"Miss Barfield," Creeger said, touching his right hand to his temple in a soft salute.

"Captain Creeger," she replied.

Creeger led the way down the hall with a purposeful stride. When Lassiter and Miss Barfield were safely far behind, Creeger turned to Langford as they continued walking. "Carl, I want you to pick five good investigators and five outstanding ones," Creeger said.

Langford nodded. "Right, Chief."

"Miss Mackenzie, I want you to pull together a list of supplies and equipment, and see if you can't gin up an estimated budget to run a staff of ten field investigators, one senior investigator," he pointed to Langford, "a records officer, one junior, and one senior," he pointed to Miss Mackenzie, "secretary, and one righteously indignant Air Force captain," Creeger said, jabbing his own chest. "You may have to get some details from Eunice the Hygienist back there." Creeger jerked his thumb over his shoulder.

Miss Mackenzie laughed warmly. "I can handle her, sir," she said.

"Congratulations on your promotions, both of you. I want all this on my desk by zero-nine-thirty tomorrow," Creeger said.

"Yes, sir."

"Will do, Chief."

"Good," Creeger said with a firm nod, pulling the brim of his crush cap over his eyes as he shoved the main door open and emerged into the light. "Oh, and Miss Mackenzie."

"Yes, sir."

"Schedule a meeting for me with General Horn, would you please?" Creeger asked. "Earliest possible convenience after ten-hundred hours tomorrow."

Miss Mackenzie smiled broadly as they rounded the

corner. "Yes sir."

Paul Lagasse is a freelance technical and feature writer whose young-adult historical novel Seeing Through Clouds *was published in 2006. He is currently researching a middle-grade historical novel set in the Baltimore neighborhood of Canton during the late 1920s. About this chapter, Paul says, "This is a scene from a novel-in-progress called 'Invasion of the Orb Men.' It is set in 1950, on the sprawling reservation of Wright Patterson Air Force Base in western Ohio, shortly after the start of the Korean War. Captain Len Creeger, a World War II veteran recalled to active duty as an intelligence officer, has just been assigned by his superior, General Horn, to take over the Air Force's investigation of 'flying saucers,' which is called Project Grudge. Creeger suspects that he's being pushed into a dead-end assignment because of his criticism of Air Force intelligence-gathering methods. The characters and setting are fictional, but the historical details about the project—and the flying saucer stories—are all authentic. I can't help wondering if Creeger's real-life counterpart felt like Creeger did when he got this job."*

The future of publishing...today!

Apprentice House is the country's only campus-based, student-staffed book publishing company. Directed by professors and industry professionals, it is a nonprofit activity of the Communication Department at Loyola College in Maryland.

Using state-of-the-art technology and an experiential learning model of education, Apprentice House publishes books in untraditional ways. This dual responsibility as publishers and educators creates an unprecedented collaborative environment among faculty and students, while teaching tomorrow's editors, designers, and marketers.

Outside of class, progress on book projects is carried forth by the AH Book Publishing Club, a co-curricular campus organization supported by Loyola College's Office of Student Activities.

Student Project Team for *Freshly Squeezed*:

Deirdre Darragh, '08
Brielle Fiorillo, '08

Eclectic and provocative, Apprentice House titles intend to entertain as well as spark dialogue on a variety of topics.

Contributions are welcomed to sustain the press's work and are tax deductible to the fullest extent allowed by the IRS. To learn more about Apprentice House books or to obtain submission guidelines, please visit www.ApprenticeHouse.com (made possible by the generous support and creativity of Mission Media).

Apprentice House
c/o Communication Department
Loyola College in Maryland
4501 N. Charles Street
Baltimore, MD 21210
Ph: 410-617-5265
Fax: 410-617-5040
info@apprenticehouse.com